Every Day is a Payday in the Kingdom of God

…A Roadmap from

Poverty to Wealth

By Yolanda Washington-Cowan

Unless otherwise indicated, scriptures are taken from the
New International Version (NIV)

Every Day is a
Payday in the Kingdom of God
...A Roadmap from Poverty to Wealth

Copyright @ 2018

ISBN-13: 978-0-9997776-3-3
ISBN-10: 0-9997776-3-7

All rights reserved

Published by
B-Inspired Publishing
7285 Winchester Road, Suite 109
Memphis, TN 38125
www.B-Inspiredpub.com
Printed in the United States
First Edition: June 2018

All rights reserved under International Copyright Law. Contents and/or cover may not be reproduced in whole or in part in any form without the expressed written consent of the Publisher.

ACKNOWLEDGEMENTS

A special thanks to my husband, Vaughn Cowan, my mother Delores and son Kenneth, Jr for their love, support, and encouragement.

Also, thanks to Alecia Robinson-Newson for editing and proofreading, and having patience in assisting me with this book.

PREFACE

Having grown up in poverty, I understand the impact it can have on people's lives. Back when I was a young girl picking up aluminum cans off the streets to make some pocket change, I realized that not having money can set limits on a person's chances of future success.

The experiences of my childhood, my parents and neighbors brought that harsh truth about poverty home to me. Financial lack is a force that devastates people's worth and purpose. It can strip a person of self-belief, autonomy and any opportunities to live a meaningful life.

Comparing my life with children in my neighborhood, at school and in church, I was able to see the difference having money made in the lives of people. I realized quite early that I had to do something to avoid being locked in a prison of poverty for the rest of my life.

In order to make that dream come true, I worked all the time. Even while I was in high school, I kept two jobs; learning how to juggle my time between studying and working. As a result, I often missed school events and could not participate in many of the activities my schoolmates did.

As I got older, I found that my pursuit, driven by the love of money, led me down a road that caused me to make bad decisions that I later had to repent for. The quest to have more and more money caused me to lose valuable relationships, miss out on important family events, and once-in-a-lifetime opportunities.

At this stage in my life, this is when I began to realize that there had to be a way to gain eternal and earthly wealth which did not force me to violate the things that I valued the most; God's words, family and my integrity.

As I grew spiritually in the word of God; I started to see that His plan for me was not to harm me but to prosper and give me a long-lived future with hope **(Jeremiah 29:11).** I began to search for a proven Bible-based pathway to prosperity and scriptures that would help me build my faith in God's promises. I also began depending on the Holy Spirit's guidance and direction to lead me from the road of poverty to wealth.

The lessons I learned on that journey are what I have documented in this book. I discovered that Every day is a Payday in the Kingdom of God and that God not only wants His children to succeed and prosper, He also has a method He has designed for them to do so.

This book is based on sound scriptural principles that will help anyone who believes in God to become a force for good by realizing their purpose, as long as they are willing to work hard. It will arm you with the knowledge that you need to not only become successful but a custodian of God's wealth in your generation.

I invite you to follow me on this exciting journey of learning and becoming all that God wants us to be.

Thank you.

Yolanda Washington-Cowan

INTRODUCTION

The Bible refers to the person who believes in Jesus as the 'light of the world.' Yet there are millions of God's people whose lives are very far from being a light to the world. Their experience of life is no different from that of non-believers around them. This is especially true of our finances; a lot of believers have money problems.

As of today, poverty is the greatest dehumanizing force on the planet. Financial lack regularly brings people to a place where they think they are worth less than a few dollars and are ready to do unimaginable things to have a little money in their pockets. Poverty is the number one driver of crime, family collapse, and social disturbance.

Poverty is far worse for those who chose to live right. It is very hard to do the right thing and still suffer. Yet this is the sad reality for hundreds of thousands of Christians everywhere around the world. As a result, many church people have come to the conclusion that being a believer excludes them from prosperity and that their blessings are reserved for them in heaven.

Why is there so much poverty in the world? Why do children have to go to bed hungry, night after night? And why does a good God permit a few people to live in mind-boggling poverty while millions of others grovel in nauseating poverty? Is there any way for good people to become wealthy without compromising their beliefs?

These are the questions that this book answers. It begins by addressing the issue of the causes of poverty and provides convincing answers to the lies that are perpetuated about why people actually suffer. Using bible-based arguments and common-sense reasoning the author un-covers the roots of global poverty and personal suffering.

Building on that, the Author debunks the false belief that God does not want His children to be materially successful. The Author shows how financial prosperity is inseparably connected to one's ability to exercise influence. By Explaining that increasing Godly influence is the most important way believers can expand the Kingdom into their neighborhoods and nations.

Using seldom discussed biblical principles; the rest of the book dedicates itself to the purpose of wealth and the right use of our material resources. It makes a distinction between materialism and blessedness. By elaborating on the character, relationship, intellectual and spiritual qualities that the believer needs to pursue while acquiring to become prosperous according to God's plan.

Every day is a Payday in the Kingdom of God is guaranteed to change the way you think about Godly wealth. It will teach you to give money its legitimate place in your life; owning it rather than being owned by it. Following the principles and steps outlined in this book will provide focus to your pursuit of wealth and balance to your life.

I challenge you to faithfully apply everything it teaches and watch God work miracles in your life!

TABLE OF CONTENTS

PREFACE	iv
INTRODUCTION	1
TABLE OF CONTENTS	8
CHAPTER ONE: GOD'S PLAN FOR YOUR LIFE	9
The Impact of Poverty	10
Poverty Destroys Love	10
Provision Creates Power	11
Poverty Prevents Purpose	11
Poverty Impairs Self-image	12
Poverty Leaves Us Defenseless	13
Poverty Destroys Morality	13
Does God Care About Me?	14
The Source of Pain	16
God's Plan For You	17
CHAPTER TWO: THE GREATEST PAYDAY	21
He Saves Our Minds	25
He Saves Our Bodies	26
He Saves Us From Poverty and Failure	27
He Saves Us From Demonic Oppression	29
He Saves Us From Purposeless Living	30
Make A Decision Today	32

CHAPTER THREE: TRUE PROSPERITY 33

   Dimensions of Prosperity 34

   What Is True Prosperity? 38

   The Prosperity of Joseph 39

   Abundant Living 43

CHAPTER FOUR: PRINCIPLES OF GODLY WEALTH 50

God's Principles of Wealth 47

   Principle #1: Purpose 48

   Principle #2: A Garden and a Seed 50

   Principle #3: Work 52

   Principle #4: Gifts 53

   Principle #5: People 55

   Principle #6: Process 56

CHAPTER FIVE: KEYS TO KINGDOM WEALTH 58

   Key #1: The Seasons for Success 58

      Characteristics of Seasons 60

   Key #2: Seedtime and Harvest 61

      Law #1: We Must Plant Something To Harvest Something 64

      Law #2: We Reap The Same As What We Sowed 64

Law #3: Our Harvest Does Not Come In The Season We Planted	65
Law #4: We Receive Back More Than We Planted	65
Law #5: Our Harvest Is In Proportion To What We Sow	66
Law #6: Good Seeds Need Constant Nurture, Bad Seeds Grow On Their Own	66
Law #7: Do Not Fret About Yesterday's Harvest, Focus on Tomorrow's Sowing	67
CHAPTER SIX: EVERYTHING BEGINS WITH A SEED	67
Understanding Your Seeds	68
The Seeds of Thoughts	68
The Seeds of Words	70
Seeds of Actions	72
Seeds of Giving	74
Finding The Right Field	77
Field# 1: Relationships	77
Field #2: Your Own Business	79
Field #3: Charitable Deeds	80
Field #4: God's Kingdom	81
CHAPTER SEVEN: DIVINE BLUEPRINT FOR WEALTH; GOD'S PART	84
God's Promise To Prosper Us	86
God's Part: The Blessing	87

An Enlightened Mind	88
Gifts, Abilities and Inspired Ideas	90
Man's Part	92
CHAPTER EIGHT: DIVINE BLUEPRINT FOR WEALTH; YOUR PART	**94**
The Tithe	95
Offerings	98
Vows	99
Where To Give Tithes and Offerings	101
The Principle of Exchange	102
Acts of Charity	104
CHAPTER NINE: STEWARDSHIP	**107**
Cultivating The Character of A Steward	109
The Qualities of a Steward	111
Trustworthiness	111
Loyalty	111
Accountability	112
Skillful	112
Moderation	112
Benefits of Good Financial Stewardship	113
CHAPTER TEN: ROADBLOCKS TO YOUR PAYDAY	**117**
Spiritual Roadblocks	117

Relationship Roadblocks	121
Developmental Roadblocks	124
Lifestyle Roadblocks	126
CHAPTER ELEVEN: TRUSTING GOD FOR YOUR PAYDAY	**129**
The Gateway to Your Payday	129
Avoiding Breakdowns On The Journey	132
It Is A Process	134
Do Not Pull Up Your Seeds	136
CHAPTER TWELVE: PRAYERS FOR PROSPERITY	**141**
CHAPTER THIRTEEN: PAYDAY CONFESSION SCRIPTURES	**147**
About The Author	151

CHAPTER ONE: GOD'S PLAN FOR YOUR LIFE

What is the single biggest issue confronting most people today? The simple answer is money; the majority people are struggling to meet their most basic needs - food, clothing and housing. Almost everyone you meet is struggling to survive. Lack is so common that it is taken for granted; most people have always struggled and the idea of having enough is alien to their thinking. In spite of this, it is very hard to live in poverty. Especially when you see other people around you living the good life and enjoying the fine things you only dare dream of. And when you realize that most poor people are not asking for a lot - just the power to put a smile on their families' faces - poverty begins to reveal itself as a real evil. Poverty can destroy the best things about people. It is hard to be poor and hold up your head in dignity. It is hard to be poor and have other people respect your opinions. Poverty takes away your ability to show your loved ones how much you care.

> They thrust the needy from the path and force all the poor of the land into hiding.
> **Job 24:4 (NIV)**

Life without the means to meet your needs and the ability to reach your goals is like a prison. There is hardly anything that you and I want to do or be in life that does not require us to have money. Your destiny and happiness are tied to your prosperity. When people are unable to meet their daily needs; their lives begin to lose meaning. This is because money is the most tangible way to measure the amount of control we have over our lives. When you have the money to change apartments or neighborhoods any time you want, you feel in control of your life. If you can choose your diet and not have to eat junk because it is cheap, you have control. Having money gives you choices and having choices gives you control and being in control gives you power. That is why when you do not have money you feel impotent. It is no coincidence that poor neighborhoods have violence; it is often because the people in them are trying to regain their lost sense of personal power.

The most important need of the human heart is for significance. Significance comes from being loved, feeling powerful and leading a meaningful life. It is very hard to feel significant when you cannot meet your basic needs. A person who is homeless does not feel loved; they feel rejected and can become depressed. The fact of having no place that they can call their own and a family that loves them is enough to drive people insane. Added to this is the way other people, including the government, treat the homeless. If a homeless person goes missing, there is no one to report it because there is no one who misses them. If a person is not missed in their absence, then they cannot consider themselves to be loved. If a person is not loved, they will not think that they matter as a human being. People need to feel that they matter but poverty can prevent that.

The Impact of Poverty

Poverty Destroys Love

Sacrifice is the first proof of love that humans demand. As infants, we began to believe that our parents loved us because of the extent of their sacrifice for us; they allowed us access to their bodies, gave us undivided attention, spent their money on us and would share their meals with us, even though we had already eaten ours. A child who is given nothing could never believe that it was loved. As adults we measure the love of others by how much they are willing to give of themselves to us. Through his generosity, women constantly test a man's love before committing to marriage. The most basic way that we define love is the willingness to share our belongings. We could never believe that someone loved us if they allowed us to suffer when they held the power to change it. Giving is the physical means by which love is communicated and poverty destroys the ability of people to give to each other.

> Dear children, let us not love with words or speech but with actions and in truth. **1 John 3:18 (NIV)**

Provision Creates Power

Money in the pocket puts a song in a person's hearts and a spring in their steps. If you have ever been without, then you understand the elation that comes with having some money in your hands. That money spells freedom; it creates a sense of power. Money in the pocket brings relief; suddenly you can smile and look to the days ahead without fear. This power is multiplied several times over when you know what to do to keep on earning money. Humans were created to be free, but it is impossible to be free if you lack the power to choose how you want to live. The simplest definition of freedom is to have options. A person who has options cannot be imposed on, because they can always leave. Many people live in neighborhoods they hate, work for bosses they detest and stay in relationships that hurt because they feel like they have no options. Poverty is a chain that binds people to a place that they hate.

Poverty Prevents Purpose

Somebody has said 'it is hard to change the world when you cannot pay your bills.' Many of us have dreams of what we would like to do with our lives, but are held back by the fear of tomorrow. We think 'where will my food, shelter, and clothes come from? Money is the biggest factor preventing people from pursuing their destiny. Not the money to make the dream come to pass, but money to meet our daily needs. It is hard to pursue purpose if you have not settled the question of provision. The thought of loved ones going to bed hungry, wearing faded old clothes and unable to go to school is enough to make the most passionate visionary shelve their dreams. Since happiness is partly tied to our purpose, this is one of the reasons most people are miserable. They feel their lives lack meaning, so they look for self-importance in other places. More often their misery is transferred as anger against their loved ones resulting in damaged relationships.

Poverty Impairs Self-image

When people are unable to meet the daily needs for themselves and love ones, how they view themselves change. They begin to see themselves as less valuable and undeserving of respect. The most precious quality a person can possess is their self-image. People want to view themselves as worthy and to be so considered by others. Our self-image is what frames our interactions and the personal boundaries that determine our sense of right and wrong. Once positive self-image is destroyed or impaired, people begin to act in uncharacteristic ways. This is one of the reasons many men begin to act strangely when they lose their jobs and can no longer provide for their families. Losing your positive self-image is like losing your way and will lead people to search in the wrong places to restore themselves. They may look to alternative sources like drugs or violence. Having money, however, can be a real boost to a person's self-image.

> The poor are shunned by all their relatives—
> how much more do their friends avoid them!
> Though the poor pursue them with pleading,
> they are nowhere to be found. **Proverbs 19:7 (NIV)**

Poverty Leaves Us Defenseless

Poverty creates vulnerability but money can buy protection. It is difficult to be poor and protect your rights. It is almost impossible to be poor and get what you deserve. This is because there are always people waiting to take away what belongs to you. If people feel they can hurt you and get away with it, they are more likely to. This is usually why the worst kinds of atrocities are committed in poor neighborhoods, and against poor people. Poverty takes away a person's voice and makes them impotent. In a world filled with injustice and violence, poverty is synonymous with weakness. This reality is what drives many young men to do desperate things to get money. They recognize that the only way to get respect and protect themselves is to have money. Others who cannot get money turn to violence because it is the only recourse they have to get justice for the wrongs they and their loved ones suffer.

> The wealth of the rich is their fortified city, but poverty is the ruin of the poor. **Proverbs 10:15 (NIV)**

Poverty Destroys Morality

It is hard to be poor and stay good. Some people will hold on to their values and beliefs regardless of their circumstances. Most people do not have that kind of inner strength. There are fathers who have had to steal because their children were hungry at home. There are also mothers who have been forced to sell their bodies to buy drugs for a sick child. These people are not thieves or prostitutes, but parents who were driven to go against their own values by lack of money. Poverty weakens personal resolve and makes it easier for a person to do wrong. It is hard for parents to convince their children to do what is right when doing what is right has not put money in the pockets of the parents. How can you convince these young people that it pays to be good, when can see gangsters, pimps, drug-pushers and street-walkers living a better life than law-abiding citizens?

> Keep falsehood and lies far from me; give me neither poverty nor riches, but give me only my daily bread. Otherwise, I may have too much and disown you and say, 'Who is the Lord?' Or I may become poor and steal, and so dishonor the name of my God. **Proverbs 30:8-9 (NIV)**

Does God Care About Me?

Many of us are asking these questions, "Why does God allow people to suffer?" "If God is as great and as powerful as the preachers say, then He can change the world with a snap of His fingers. Why does He not?" "Or maybe God does not just care about us." These are questions people ask every day and they have good reason to. It is not easy to see how God can love people with all of the suffering in the world. It is tempting to believe instead that He does not care or even worse, that God likes to see people suffer. Yet, it does not make sense to believe that God loves to see us suffer; because there are too many things in life that show us that this is not true. All around us is evidence that proves that the God who created the world loves people and wants them to be happy and well. Take a moment to think about the world around you.

> The Lord loves righteousness and justice;
> the earth is full of his unfailing love. **Psalm 33:5 (NIV)**

Why do the sunset, stars and forest have to be beautiful? Why do birds and insects come in so many breathtaking varieties? The world is beautiful because its creator loves the ones He created to live in it and wants to delight them with its beauty. The same way a parent enjoys watching a toddler playing in the rain or snow for the first time. Why is there so much abundance wired into the earth? When plants produce, they make more seeds and fruits than they need. When fish multiply, they make swarms of fries and still the oceans are able to accommodate and feed them. The earth hates emptiness so much that any empty place is soon colonized by plants and animals. God loves abundance not poverty. Only a good God could create happiness and arrange that people are only happy when they are making others happy. Only a God who loves people would create us to need one another. Only a loving God could create love. A cruel God would never do such things.

> Every good and perfect gift is from above, coming down from the Father of the heavenly lights, who does not change like shifting shadows. **James 1:17 (NIV)**

Think about how vitalizing cold water can be on a warm summer day or the delight of having a loved one scratch that unreachable itch? Those are insignificant pleasures that only a God Who cares about people would make. Or consider the ringing laughter of small children in the playground and the shameless grin of a toothless infant. Things that reach into the soul in ways that word cannot describe. What about the infinite variety of fruits and the rich sweetness of squeezing their ripe juice into your mouth? These are not the creations of a God who hates people. God is a happy God; only a happy person spreads happiness. Only a happy God would infuse such happiness into His world. Why do people have to tickle? Or is there any purpose to laughter other than happiness? Everywhere we look in the world we see animals at play; dolphins, puppies and bears - because that is the Kind of God who created the world.

> For the Lord God is a sun and shield; the Lord bestows favor and honor; no good thing does he withhold from those whose walk is blameless. **Psalm 84:11 (NIV)**

> … put their hope in God, who richly provides us with everything for our enjoyment. **1 Timothy 6:17 (NIV)**

The Source of Pain

> What causes fights and quarrels among you? Don't they come from your desires that battle within you? You desire but do not have, so you kill. You covet but you cannot get what you want, so you quarrel and fight. **James 4:1-2 (NIV)**

If God is good, then where does the pain in the world come from? It does not come from God; suffering is alien to God's plan for the world. Pain and suffering happen when the desires of God are contradicted by people. When people ask why God permits pain and suffering, they never think of pains and sufferings in terms of what they themselves do. They view pain and suffering as the result of another person's actions. It does not occur to us that our action in our small corner of the world is part of the massive pain and sufferings that is suffocating the world. We view our own wrongdoing as insignificant little pebbles compared to the huge mountains of injustice around us. But if all seven billion people on the planet are throwing pebbles at one another, those pebbles quickly become a hailstorm of trouble falling on everything and everyone. The troubles in the world are the sum-total of the insignificant acts of pain that each of us carries out against another person. We, not God, are the ones killing the world.

> Why do you look at the speck of sawdust in your brother's eye and pay no attention to the plank in your own eye? How can you say to your brother, 'Let me take the speck out of your eye,' when all the time there is a plank in your own eye? You hypocrite, first take the plank out of your own eye, and then you will see clearly to remove the speck from your brother's eye. **Matthew 7:3-5 (NIV)**

Human beings are generally self-righteous and hypocritical. We obsess over other people's wrongdoings and think of them as the problem. We point fingers at those people stealing billions, but never at our own petty dishonesties. We accuse governments and corporations of starting wars, while ignoring the emotional violence we perpetrate against our families. The problem is with the racists and Nazis, and never with our gossiping, back-stabbing and malice. The responsibility is out there and never in here. But Jesus taught that the change we want to see in others begins with an adjustment of our own attitudes and actions. He says that the errors of other people will become less of a problem as we deal with our own faults. There is pain and suffering in the world because there is hate and greed in people. If we want to see a better world, we must become better ourselves. And as long as everyone is waiting for somebody to start it, nobody is going to do it.

> This only have I found: God created mankind upright, but they have gone in search of many schemes. **Ecclesiastes 7:29 (NIV)**

God's Plan For You

> The Lord is my shepherd, I lack nothing. **Psalm 23:1 (NIV)**

> The Lord your God has blessed you in all the work of your hands. He has watched over your journey through this vast wilderness. These forty years the Lord your God has been with you, and you have not lacked anything. **Deuteronomy 2:7 (NIV)**

But regardless of what has gone wrong with the world, God still has a plan for us, if we submit to Him and follow His commandments. The desire of God for all humanity has never stopped being that you and I should be happy, healthy and fully provided for. Even though that plan has been obscured by the willfulness of humans, it remains intact and God is fully committed to making it work for anyone who obeys Him. Every good parent bringing a child into the world prepares for them. They anticipate the needs of that child and provide for them. Even before a child knows that it will need something, the parents are already working to have it ready. God is no different; in fact, He does much better for His children. He has gone ahead of us to prepare all the resources we will ever need for our physical, mental, emotional and spiritual well-being. All He demands of us is that we follow Him, so that He can walk us into that provision.

> God saw all that he had made, and it was very good. And there was evening, and there was morning—the sixth day. **Genesis 1:31 (NIV)**

In the book of Genesis, when God made us, He declared that man was good. In other words, God had ensured that we possessed all the physical resources we would need to make a success of our lives. God has said about you that 'you are good' - that means that you are sufficient for all that you were created for. You have been specifically built and equipped to succeed in life. The mental, emotional, and

spiritual faculties that are necessary to reach the place of sufficiency and happiness have been built into you are at your disposal. The beginning of understanding God's plan for you is to embrace this knowledge that you are sufficient for the life that you are made to live. Just as when a baby emerges from the womb, the midwife first checks that the baby is alive, breathing. Next, she examines every part of the baby's body to ensure that it is complete. In the same way, when God first made humans, he examined them and declared them fit for their purpose.

> Now the Lord God had planted a garden in the east, in Eden; and there he put the man he had formed. The Lord God made all kinds of trees grow out of the ground—trees that were pleasing to the eye and good for food. In the middle of the garden were the tree of life and the tree of the knowledge of good and evil. **Genesis 2:8-9 (NIV)**

After God had satisfied Himself that Adam was adequate for the purpose for which he was created, God began to assemble to Adam all the material things He would need to make his life a success. God first guaranteed that Adam and Eve were capable, now He began to make sure that they were supplied with everything they needed to fulfill their assignment. God did not expect them to go and find their own food and shelter; He provided those things to them. Looking for what to eat and where to live is not the job that God gave to humans. It is not meant to be the pursuit that dominates our whole lives. As long as Adam and Eve were living in obedience to God and pursuing His purpose for their lives, their physical needs became God's responsibility. In the same way that it is the employer's responsibility to give the employee everything they need to do the job.

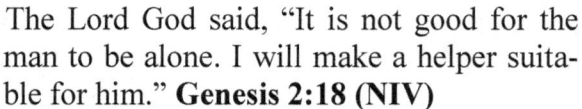

> The Lord God said, "It is not good for the man to be alone. I will make a helper suitable for him." **Genesis 2:18 (NIV)**

Finally, God provided for Adam's relationship needs. Before Adam even realized that he would need a mate, God went about finding a partner for Adam. This shows that God is not only aware of our relational and sexual needs; He will make provision for those needs to be fully satisfied. In short, God's plan is that we enjoy well-being in every dimension of our being. He not only wants us to prosper materially, He also wants us to thrive physically, mentally and emotionally. He wants your life to have meaning. He wants you to have relationships that validate you. God wants you to be complete and happy in every dimension of your existence. That was His plan from the beginning and it is still His plan today. What changed was man, not God. God promises that if we come back to His original place and purpose for us, we will find His original plan intact waiting for us.

> For I know the plans I have for you," declares the LORD, "plans to prosper you and not to harm you, plans to give you hope and a future. **Jeremiah 29:11 (NIV)**

CHAPTER TWO: THE GREATEST PAYDAY

The key to returning to God's original plan for your life and my life is to come back to living as God originally intended for us too. People never ask themselves what purpose the creator had in mind when He created them. If people did not make themselves, people cannot determine the reason for their own existence. This is a natural law which is not hard to understand. The maker always decides what their product or invention is meant to do. This is why it is always the cook who says what the food is. We do not ask the food, because the cook holds the recipe. When humans build something, they always define its purpose. The same is true of God; He determines what our purpose is and prescribed the best methods for fulfilling that purpose. The happiness we experience is dependent on our following His plan.

The sufferings and pains in the world are caused by humanity wandering from their creator's intention for their lives. Just like every manufacturer would, God has been trying to fix people for centuries. But unlike a piece of equipment, people have a will and can choose if they want to be repaired or not. God created you and me with a free will which He will not violate; He only fixes people if they allow Him to work in their lives. This is why it is not possible for God to merely snap His finger and change the world. Expecting Him to do this is asking Him to disregard our freedom of choice. That would make God no different than tyrants and neighborhood bullies who routinely force their will on other people. God's unwillingness to change the world by force is the assurance that you and I have that He will never use His great power to dominate us. As humans, we dread being subjugated; that is why God lets us choose our path.

> Come to me, all you who are weary and burdened, and I will give you rest. **Matthew 11:28 (NIV)**

Although God allows you and me to choose the path we want to follow, He does not give us control over the consequences of our choices. He only forewarns us that if we go against what He commands, there will be negative outcomes. We may choose to play naked in the rain, but we cannot negotiate with the cold. We can choose to jump off the cliff, but we cannot control what gravity does with us. Every action we take is a cause that creates an effect and the effects often occur in ways that we cannot predict. Like children playing with fire, we do not control what the fire burns or does not burn. Unlike in movies there is no time machine to transport us back in time to change things. The only way to control any outcome is to not take the action that leads to it. If we do not play with fire, there is no risk of burning down the house. This is why God urges us to obey His words - it is to protect us, not to control us.

> This day I call the heavens and the earth as witnesses against you that I have set before you life and death, blessings and curses. Now choose life, so that you and your children may live **Deuteronomy 30:19 (NIV)**

You and I have a choice to continue to live in rebellion along with the majority of humanity. Or we can submit to God's will and allow Him to begin to lead us out of the self-destructive ways we have lived in. Our journey to peace and prosperity begins with submitting to God. This means that we have to recognize that someone created this world and fixed the rules for living in it. If we want to have a good experience living on earth, we must live according to His principles. When we do this, we automatically switch camps; from being part of those humans destroying the world, we become one of those restoring it. From that point onwards, God begins to work in us; first to change us internally, then to improve the results that we have been getting in our lives, and finally, to make us agents of change to the world around us.

This experience is what the Bible refers to as being saved. We are saved from the foolish ideas that we have lived by, saved from the consequences of our wrong lifestyles and saved from the judgment of God against all those who disobey Him. This salvation is the greatest gift that God could ever give to mankind because we are totally undeserving of it. We have all, at one time, been given a chance to do what is right but we have mostly intentionally chosen to do wrong because we enjoyed it and it offered us some advantage. Yet, God does not hold this willful wrong-doing against us; rater he offers us a second chance if we obey Him today; an opportunity to start again on a clean slate. God does not do this because He is nonchalant about sin and can easily wave it away. He does it because in His love for people, He has found a way to help us escape the painful consequences of our misconduct.

> But God demonstrates his own love for us in this: While we were still sinners, Christ died for us. **Romans 5:8 (NIV)**

> The Lord is not slow in keeping his promise, as some understand slowness. Instead he is patient with you, not wanting anyone to perish, but everyone to come to repentance. **2 Peter 3:9 (NIV)**

In the same way that a manufacturer consigns every product which does not meet with his specifications to destruction, God punishes rebellion with death. This death is not merely to stop breathing because even when we stop breathing, we do not stop living. Humans are spirits and when we die; our spirits merely leave our bodies and keep on existing. This death means that even after the death of our physical bodies, our spirits, the real us will continue to suffer. Everything that is the opposite of what makes us alive is what that spirit will endure. That person will live without light, peace, joy, love, laughter, quiet, rest, friendship and everything that represents life and happiness. They will endure an eternity of torment since they rejected what is right and good, and chose destruction and darkness while they lived on earth. God has provided that if we obey Him today, even if we have sinned in the past, we can escape this fate.

By providing Jesus as a substitute to suffer the punishments of our sins, God offers us the chance to escape His judgment without breaking His own law. It is similar to the story of the son of a judge who is brought before his own father for a traffic offense. That judge subjected himself to the requirements of the law and fined his son as he would other offenders. Afterwards, he provided his son with the money to pay the fine, in order to keep him from going to prison. That father did not let his love for his son interfere with justice but he also did not allow justice prevent him from loving his son. By sending Jesus to offer us a way out of our predicament, God shows His love. At the same time, He upholds His righteous law, in order to show us that He always does what He says. That way He provides us with two strong pillars upon which to build our confidence in Him; His love and His dependability.

> He sent His word and healed them, and rescued them from their destruction. **Psalm 107:20 (AMP)**

God's salvation is not just about Him saving us from His judgment, it is much more. In the beginning, when God created the first humans, His provision for them covered every dimension of their existence. He made sure that they were physically and mentally whole. He provided adequate housing and food for them. He gave them relationships to meet their emotional needs and also gave meaning to their lives. When mankind walked away from God's plan and suffered as a result, the consequences of their disobedience also impacted on every aspect of their lives. It touched their bodies with sickness, their families with pain, their minds with foolishness and their wealth with scarcity. It makes sense therefore that God's salvation for us should encompass all these areas. When we come back to God, it should affect our health, minds, relationships and possessions. That is exactly the case; God's salvation is total.

He Saves Our Minds

When God was about to make man He said, 'Let us make man in our own Image.' This meant that man had the same basic character and insights as God had, but on a smaller level. Man could communicate and reason with God because his spirit was alive and his mind was enlightened. He was capable of grasping the truths of God; he could think through issues using the principles of God and arrive at conclusions that were consistent with God's thoughts. However, when man sinned, his spirit was disconnected from God and his soul was cut off from the insights of God. He lost his ability to see straight and think correctly. As a result, human thinking became twisted and futile. People were unable to see the stupidity of their ways because they reasoned with a twisted logic. This is why people keep making the same mistakes over and over; they do not fully perceive the world around them.

> So I tell you this, and insist on it in the Lord,
> that you must no longer live as the Gentiles

do, in the futility of their thinking. **Ephesians 4:17 (NIV)**

For you have spent enough time in the past doing what pagans choose to do—living in debauchery, lust, drunkenness, orgies, carousing and detestable idolatry. They are surprised that you do not join them in their reckless, wild living, and they heap abuse on you. **1 Peter 4:3-4 (NIV)**

When we come to God, He begins the reconstruction of our minds. He brings His light back into our spirits and we are able to access the insights of God. We have at our disposal God's viewpoint on issues. That viewpoint is based on perfect knowledge and it furnishes us with the ability to make the right choices. It allows us to see clearly; we can discern where a course of action will ultimately lead and avoid it. We begin to let go of the foolish notions and false assumptions we held about ourselves and the world. Our way of thinking and our actions become more consistent with reality and we stop living by our instincts. We are guided by God's truth and the reality of what is around us, rather than being blown about by the loudest voice or the emotion of the moment. As the Bible says 'He restores our soul.'

He Saves Our Bodies

The plan of God for us has never included sickness. Sickness and disease occur when our bodies fail to function as God intended that they should. This could be the result of many things, but whatever the cause of ill-health; it is always an obstacle which prevents people from living out God's purpose for them. Just as sin is a disruption of the proper way our minds should function, disease is a violation of the correct way our bodies should function. When cancer occurs in a person, it is because the cells of their body act in ways that they should not. When people die of AIDS, it is because something foreign takes control of the body and destroys it. All sickness is a violation of God's order and purpose. It is not just a problem for mankind; it is also God's problem because it frustrates His plans. This is why God has always given physical health and the healing of diseases a special place in His relationship with people.

> He himself bore our sins in his body on the cross, so that we might die to sins and live for righteousness; by his wounds you have been healed. **1 Peter 2:24 (NIV)**

Jesus spent a considerable part of His life healing the sick. The Bible also says that He died to secure physical healing for our bodies. This means that in both His life and death, Jesus was dedicated to the physical well-being of people. That is how much importance God places on your physical well-being. He knows that you cannot have a healthy mind if your body is sick. He understands that it is impossible to make and enjoy wealth unless you are free of sickness and disease. He also recognizes that you will not reap the full benefits of your relationships if you are in a hospital bed. In order for us to have sound minds, be strong enough to build wealth and capable of freely loving others, we have to be well in our bodies. God's salvation makes full provision not just for the healing of our bodies but for us to continue to live in good health.

> Nevertheless, I will bring health and healing to it; I will heal my people and will let them enjoy abundant peace and security. **Jeremiah 33:6 (NIV)**

He Saves Us From Poverty and Failure

Poverty is a strategy the enemy uses to hold you back from God's plan for your life. In the beginning, God gave humans dominion, but it is impossible to exercise dominion if one is poor. To have dominion means to exert influence and exercise power. It is the ability to have a say in how things are done. A person with no money hardly has a say in what happens in his or her own life, speak less of being able to determine how their city is run. Money offers us a platform for gaining the respect and attention of people. The more money a group of people have, the more they are able to influence the world around them. It is not enough to have good intentions, what matters for achieving actual progress is power. And money creates power. This is why after God made man; He gave him property; a place to live in and a garden to work in. By providing him a home and a business, God gave him tangible tools for growing and expanding his influence.

> So I said, "Wisdom is better than strength."
> But the poor man's wisdom is despised, and
> his words are no longer heeded. **Ecclesiastes 9:16 (NIV)**

God recognizes that good people need money in order to demonstrate His love to the world. The Bible commands us to help the needy and defend the weak, but how can we do that if we are weak and needy ourselves? Wealth is not merely something that is nice to have; it is a vital tool for making the world a better place. Every time God gives someone an assignment, He also gives them the means to do it. Wealth is God's means for achieving God's plan for the righteous to dominate the earth. This is why God works to put wealth in the hands of the righteous, while taking it from the control of the wicked. God wants His children to prosper because it is a proof of his love and provision for them. Secondly, He knows how much good can come from having money in the hands of the right people. Thirdly, wealth, not poverty, is the true reflection of God's power and benevolence.

> For you know the grace of our Lord Jesus Christ, that though he was rich, yet for your sake he became poor, so that you through his poverty might become rich. 2 **Corinthians 8:9 (NIV)**

He Saves Us From Demonic Oppression

God did not create man to be dominated; He created him to exercise dominion. This means that we are excluded from all forms of demonic oppression. However, demons began to have power over people as a result of rebellion and sin. When man sinned, he lost his status as the agent of God's authority on the earth. Instead he became a subject in the kingdom of Satan and was now vulnerable to every attack of Satan. As a result, people became subjected to demonic oppression of every sort: mental illness, physical sickness, nightmares, uncontrollable fears, curses of financial failure, broken marriages, single parenthood, early death, etc. This domination of humans by demonic spirits was never part of God's original design, it happened as the result of humanity rebelling against God. But God has provided a way for us to not only be freed from the power of Satan but to also be restored to our place of authority.

> For he has rescued us from the dominion of darkness and brought us into the kingdom of the Son he loves. **Colossians 1:13 (NIV)**

> Since you died with Christ to the elemental spiritual forces of this world. **Colossians 2:20 (NIV)**

Christ death on the cross fully satisfied the demands of God's judgment against sin. When we accept the sacrifice of Jesus on the cross, we are delivered from the consequences of disobeying God, including oppression by satanic spirits. Through salvation, we are also restored to the place God originally intended for us; the place of dominion. As a result, the believer is elevated in authority above the Devil. He is no longer part of the Kingdom of Satan, but is now a member of the righteous army enforcing God's judgments against the Devil. Through salvation we are empowered to overcome what used to defeat us. If a person who has received Jesus as Lord and Savior still suffers from demonic oppression, that evil spirit is operating illegally. It is taking advantage of that person's ignorance to afflict them. Like a thief taking advantage of an unlocked door, the spirit is an opportunist.

> I have given you authority to trample on snakes and scorpions and to overcome all the power of the enemy; nothing will harm you. **Luke 10:19 (NIV)**

He Saves Us From Purposeless Living

> You are the salt of the earth. But if the salt loses its saltiness, how can it be made salty again? It is no longer good for anything, except to be thrown out and trampled underfoot. You are the light of the world. A town built on a hill cannot be hidden. Neither do people light a lamp and put it under a bowl. Instead they put it on its stand, and it gives light to everyone in the house. In the same way, let your light shine before others, that they may see your good deeds and glorify your Father in heaven. **Matthew 5:13-16 (NIV)**

In the beginning, God said about mankind 'let them have dominion over the earth.' This meant that the man who was carrying God's mind inside him would be the dominant influence on the earth. The result of this would be that mankind would frame everything on earth to fit into his point of view, which is God's. So as the man was imposing himself on his environment, the effect would be that the whole earth would soon become a reflection of the God who was inside that man. This is what Jesus meant when He prayed *'Your will be done on the earth, as it is in heaven.'* He meant that God's children would be the instruments to spread the knowledge and the character of God across the world. We would be making the world more and more like heaven through our thinking, actions and relationships.

In practical terms, this means that we use our position and profession to advance the principles of God. This does not mean constantly preaching to people; rather it means internalizing God's truth and reflecting it in our daily interactions with the world. Whether as a teacher, baker, shopkeeper, cab driver, nurse, entrepreneur, technician, artist, lawyer, student, parent or preacher, we conduct our business in a way that leaves people wanting to ask what makes us different. It also means dedicating our time, money and thoughts to advancing those things that promote the values of the word of God. This could be by voting, occupying a leadership position, speaking out on issues or simply not buying from businesses that fund unrighteousness. Whatever way we choose, our lives begin to be shaped by a higher purpose.

> And he died for all, that those who live should no longer live for themselves but for him who died for them and was raised again. **2 Corinthians 5:15 (NIV)**

> Let your conversation be always full of grace, seasoned with salt, so that you may know how to answer everyone. **Colossians 4:6 (NIV)**

Make A Decision Today

If you have never repented of your sins and surrendered your life to Jesus, making Him the Lord of your life, you can do so by praying the prayer below. Everything in the rest of this book rests on this one decision and may not be of much benefit to you, until you settle the issue.

You may also pray the prayer if you had at one time prayed the prayer of salvation, but failed to live up to the commitment you made.

A Prayer for Salvation

Dear God, I come to You in the Name of Jesus. Your word says that we all have sinned and fallen short of the just requirements of Your Word. Lord, I come to you as a sinner standing under your righteous judgment and I repent of my sins and I ask for mercy and forgiveness. Dear God, because of your love for me, You sent your Son, Jesus, to suffer in my place by dying on the cross for my sins. Today, I accept the sacrifice of Jesus and I ask you to wash my sins away by the blood of your son. Forgive me of my sins and cleanse me of every wrong way of thinking and living; deliver me from the power of sin. I surrender my life to your will and bring everything that belongs to me under your control. Today, I declare that I am no longer the master of my life but I accept Jesus as my savior and the Lord of my life. Lord, erase my name from the book of death and write it in Your book of life. Today, I do declare that I am saved, that I am born again by the blood of Jesus. Dear God, thank you for saving me, in the Name of your sweet Son, Jesus, I pray. Amen.

CHAPTER THREE: TRUE PROSPERITY

What is success? How you answer that question determines what you value and dedicate your life to achieving. In general terms we define success as:

> *"The realization of an aim or purpose"*
>
> *"An action that hits its intended target"*

This definition of success leaves everyone with the choice to determine what their intended *aim* or *target* is. The person who sets the goal of swindling people of their money is successful if he achieves that goal. The same is true of the politician who schemes to steal public funds, the spouse who plans to be unfaithful, the racist who plots the murder of thousands of people, the young man who wants to sleep with as many women as he can and the drug dealer who tries to get teenagers hooked on crack. If these people 'hit their intended targets' they are successful, regardless of the consequence of those successes.

So once again, what is success? Success is not just about the accomplishment of goals but also about the impact of those goals on the people around us and the world at large. If my success results in the destruction of other people's happiness or removes opportunities for them to also get what I have gotten, can that success be good? True success, by succeeding also creates grounds for the success of others. Success is not simply what I do or what I get, it is also about what others think about what I do and what I get. The failure to allow other people to have a say in what I call success is what creates war and conflict. If all of us pursued what we wanted, without giving thought to what others want, the world would be in anarchy. So, success is not just

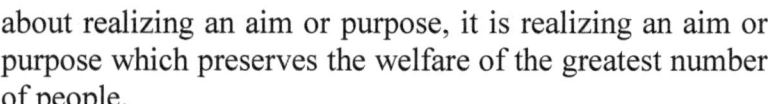

about realizing an aim or purpose, it is realizing an aim or purpose which preserves the welfare of the greatest number of people.

This definition of success is what creates the difference between the success of God and the success of Satan. The success of God satisfies not only the needs of the person chasing success; it also secures the interests of others in the world. On the other hand, the success of Satan is one-dimensional; focused only on the needs and interests of the person who seeks that success. The success of Satan is so destructive that it eventually harms even the person pursuing it. This is why the bible makes a distinction between good success and bad success. Good success is uplifting for the successful and creates liberation for others. Bad success is depressing for the successful and creates oppression for others. That is why people often curse the success of the rich; they know that their success has not helped them in any way; rather it has limited them by taking away from them.

> This Book of the Law shall not depart out of your mouth, but you shall meditate on it day and night, that you may observe and do according to all that is written in it. For then you shall make your way prosperous, and then you shall deal wisely and have good success. **Joshua 1:8 (AMPC)**

> When the righteous prosper, the city rejoices; when the wicked perish, there are shouts of joy. **Proverbs 11:10 (NIV)**

Dimensions of Prosperity

What is prosperity? This is what the dictionary says:

"flourishing or thriving condition, especially in financial respects"

or

"characterized by financial success"

In short, prosperity is to have money. That is how prosperity is defined for us in the world today. So even if a group of people - like the aborigines of many lands - do not have any money but are happy and have everything they need, they are not prosperous. Everything around us tells us that prosperity is not about being happy or having enough but about owning lots of things. We are led to believe that things will make us happy. The more things we have, the happier we will be, never mind if we need those things or not. The hidden message is that you and I are defined by how much things we buy, and how expensive and exclusive those things are. It is not enough to have good clothes, shoes, bags, phones and cars; you must have the latest products by the biggest designers. If you don't, you ought to be ashamed.

What most people refer to as prosperity is actually materialism; the habit of determining the worth of people by what they have. Materialism is a system that does not consider the inner value of people but only measures their possessions. This kind of system does not pay attention to character, even if it says it does. What counts are only things which can be counted. In this system, the best people are those who have managed to accumulate the most. Anyone who wants to be respected must prove their worth by making tons of money. In other words, money becomes the standard for measuring people. It does not matter if a person is a dishonest pervert, if he has money, he will be celebrated. The result is that people begin to feel that they are wasting time by doing the right thing and begin to abandon

their morality. In a materialistic world, people will do anything to be seen and heard.

A materialistic system places no value on the most vital aspects of human life. It elevates human greed above human need. It makes the pursuit of status more important than real happiness. It treats morality as something that can be discarded if it interferes with success. This is why in such a society people are encouraged to buy more and more things. That impulse to buy is driven by greed and fear. They do not want others to have more than they do because they fear that they will be looked down on if they do not own more stuff. It does not matter whether it is to buy more clothes or acquire more companies; the materialistic behavior is the same. It is driven by envy, greed and insecurity. The people cannot stop to ask if they need what they purchase because they are in bondage to a spirit of greed. The only thought in their minds is to get more than the next person and to show it off.

The real reason why anyone should ever buy anything is because they have a need that the thing can satisfy. Once the connection between need and what we buy is broken, what replaces it is an insane pursuit of things. People are caught in a meaningless cycle of getting things for the sake of having them. Although they do not need what they pursue, they will sacrifice anything to get it, including their own happiness. A person's highest value determines the direction of their lives. If that highest value is money, it will lead them to violate everything that stands in the way of money and status. This is why young people will submit to perverted sex or commit murder for a few thousand dollars, to get signed on to a record label or to land a role in a movie. Money has become their highest value and the praise of men, their greatest aspiration. For these things, they will sacrifice their morality and wellbeing, as well as

the happiness or lives of others. But the question is 'Is it really worth it?' 'In the end, will it actually matter?'

> What good is it for someone to gain the whole world, yet forfeit their soul? Or what can anyone give in exchange for their soul? **Mark 8:36-37 (NIV)**

> Will not all of them taunt him with ridicule and scorn, saying, '"Woe to him who piles up stolen goods and makes himself wealthy by extortion! How long must this go on?' Will not your creditors suddenly arise? Will they not wake up and make you tremble? Then you will become their prey. **Habakkuk 2:6-7** (NIV)

Jesus said that if a man acquires the world, but in the process, loses himself he has gained nothing. If in a bid to get those things which I cannot keep, I lose the one thing which I cannot buy, have I really gained anything? As a result of elevating money above everything else, people lose everything else. Those things that bear our name will only do so until we are dead; after that we no longer have a claim. The ownership of material things is an illusion because nobody can really keep anything. This is why the Bible teaches that the only profit people get from owning stuff is the pleasure of gloating over it. Therefore, things are to be used as a means to meet our needs and let go of afterwards. In place of chasing what we cannot keep, we should dedicate our lives to things that create real satisfaction and make people happy, like family and truth. We will always carry those in our souls wherever we go because they have real worth.

> As goods increase, so do those who consume them. And what benefit are they to the

owners except to feast their eyes on them? **Ecclesiastes 5:11 (NIV)**

Go, eat your food with gladness, and drink your wine with a joyful heart, for God has already approved what you do. Always be clothed in white, and always anoint your head with oil. Enjoy life with your wife, whom you love. **Ecclesiastes 9:7-9 (NIV)**

What Is True Prosperity?

True prosperity allows a person to thrive in all dimensions of their existence. It is not the one-dimensional pursuit of money, power and position that disregards wellbeing. It does not lead us to hurt people, including ourselves or disregard truth in order to get what we want. When a person seeks wealth in the way that God meant for it to be done, money is not the principal goal of their lives. Instead of elevating money to the place of God, it becomes a tool for achieving goals and not the goal. Bear in mind that a person's highest value determines the direction of their lives. Money is relegated to the role of servant and not given the place of a master. This means that we force the pursuit of money to submit and find a place behind other more important things in our lives. Money is not in the driving seat deciding when we will have time for family, how we treat people and whether we are honest or not.

True prosperity means that we place greater emphasis on achieving growth in other areas of our lives than on growing our assets. The reference point for making decisions goes from being 'how much?' or 'what do I gain?' to 'is it right?' We judge our attitudes and actions by what is right or wrong because the compass of our lives is no longer our net-worth but God's word. Instead of sacrificing our values, relationships and well-being to make money, we forgo money to preserve what is true. This allows the person to remain whole while following their goal of material prosperity. They may make money slower than the materialistic person does but what little they have will have a greater impact on their lives because it goes to meeting actual needs and they also draw happiness from others sources, other than money.

> Better a small serving of vegetables with love than a fattened calf with hatred. **Proverbs 15:17** (NIV)

The Prosperity of Joseph

> Now Joseph had been taken down to Egypt. Potiphar, an Egyptian who was one of Pharaoh's officials, the captain of the guard, bought him from the Ishmaelites who had taken him there. The Lord was with Joseph so that he prospered, and he lived in the house of his Egyptian master. When his master saw that the Lord was with him and that the Lord gave him success in everything he did, Joseph found favor in his eyes and became his attendant. Potiphar put him in charge of his household, and he entrusted to his care everything he owned. From the time he put him in charge of his household and of all that he owned, the Lord blessed the household of the Egyptian because of Joseph. The blessing of the Lord was on everything Potiphar had, both in the house and in the field. So Potiphar left everything he had in Joseph's care; with Joseph in charge, he did not concern himself with anything except the food he ate. Now Joseph was well-built and handsome, and after a while

his master's wife took notice of Joseph and said, "Come to bed with me!" But he refused. "With me in charge," he told her, "my master does not concern himself with anything in the house; everything he owns he has entrusted to my care. No one is greater in this house than I am. My master has withheld nothing from me except you, because you are his wife. How then could I do such a wicked thing and sin against God? **Genesis 39:1-9 (NIV)**

That the central thing in prosperity is not money but the person is beautifully illustrated for us in the Biblical story of Joseph. To fully grasp this story, we need to understand what slavery meant for Joseph. He had no property or identity. He was in a foreign land and most likely struggled to understand the language and culture. He was deprived and given the barest minimum necessary to keep him strong enough to do his work. Yet in the midst of these difficulties, the bible says he prospered. How could someone who had no freedom and owned no property prosper? The Bible further says that he had success in everything he did, to the point that his master noticed and set him over his household and his business. How can a person who did not even own his own life be called successful? When the Bible calls Joseph prosperous, what does it mean, given that it certainly does not mean that he had a lot of money?

He was not called prosperous because he had money. He was called prosperous because of the inner qualities he possessed. Through these inner qualities, Joseph was able to constantly experience success in his endeavors regardless of his limiting circumstances. Even though he had no money, he was constantly advancing and developing. When it says that Joseph prospered, the Bible really meant that he was developed internally and as a result of that internal development, whatever he did on the outside yielded good results. He manifested a level of effectiveness that was uncommon. He had what some people would refer to as 'the magic touch.' It allowed him to succeed where others had failed. He became so good that his master overlooked freemen and set a slave over his business. The implication is that Joseph, a slave, was set as overseer over those freemen who would have worked for his master. What gave him this edge?

Joseph pursued the success that mattered most; he set his priorities right and the rest of his life fell into shape. If money was the central goal of his life, he would have been unable to do anything in Egypt because slavery limited his options. The principal purpose of his life was to understand and submit to the will of God in his life. Secondly, he was committed to his own personal growth and development. Thirdly he cultivated a habit of maintaining good relations with people, regardless of their character. However, the most important quality that allowed Joseph to do all of these things was his commitment to retain a positive outlook despite his unfortunate circumstances. Joseph refused to submit to despair. Even though, he was a slave outwardly, he refused to become a slave inwardly. As a result, he escaped the trap that slaves fall into and rose to a level of character that was even hard to find among the free.

> To the person who pleases him, God gives wisdom, knowledge and happiness, but to the sinner he gives the task of gathering and storing up wealth to hand it over to the one who pleases God. This too is meaningless, a chasing after the wind. **Ecclesiastes 2:26 (NIV)**

Joseph prospered in his spirit, in his mind, in his hands and in his relationships. Due to Joseph thriving in his relationship with God, the Bible says that the Lord caused all that he did to succeed. Meaning that Joseph's spirituality empowered his mind and hands to achieve his goals. God imparted insight into his mind and skill to his hands. Joseph applied himself to tasks that were assigned to him until he succeeded because he was trying to please God, not get back at his master. While other slaves became bitter, angry and a pain to work with, Joseph refused to become negative. Through the combination of these factors he succeeded over and over, until he rose to the position of overseer over the whole business and was able to guide the business to achieve incredible success in record time. Joseph could be trusted because he held to a set of values which placed his internal development above his external wealth.

> Whoever loves money never has enough; whoever loves wealth is never satisfied with their income. This too is meaningless. **Ecclesiastes 5:10 (NIV)**

You and I can never be satisfied by the pursuit of things. No matter how much we have, life will always be empty if we do not give proper perspective to our pursuit of wealth. Many people try to use money to compensate for their lack of meaningful connections. They hope that the void left by lack of friendship, love and spirituality can be filled by things. It is madness to think that we can replace God with gold and people with property. The result of such an endeavor is that the person becomes even more spiritually stunted as their spirit shrivels further. The pursuit of money is a bottomless pit that leads nowhere. People are fooled into thinking that they will finally find happiness with the next deal or purchase. But it never happens. Money only acquires meaning when it is used in service of things we love and those we love; God and humanity. It is a servant, and must never be allowed to rule our lives.

Abundant Living

> The thief comes only to steal and kill and destroy; I have come that they may have life, and have it to the full. **John 10:10 (NIV)**

> And God is able to bless you abundantly, so that in all things at all times, having all that you need, you will abound in every good work. **2 Corinthians 9:8 (NIV)**

True prosperity is to live an abundant life, to thrive in every department of your being. It means that there is no deadness in you. No part of your life is in darkness. Rather you have balance and as a result you are able to bloom. Just like Adam and Eve in the garden of Eden, every part of their lives were in a state of harmony with the will of God, their own personal desires and the needs of the world around them. When a person has true prosperity, they will possess and flourish in the following areas:

- <u>God-Centered Values</u>: They will have core values that put God in the center of their lives.

> The beginning of wisdom is this: Get wisdom. Though it cost all you have, get understanding. **Proverbs 4:7 (NIV)**

- <u>Wellness in all of their faculties</u>: These include spiritual knowledge, physical health, mental alertness and aptitude

> Dear friend, I pray that you may enjoy good health and that all may go well with you, even as your soul is getting along well. **3 John 2 (NIV)**

- <u>Fulfilling Purpose</u>: Work that they love and which benefits humanity

> That each of them may eat and drink, and find satisfaction in all their toil—this is the gift of God. **Ecclesiastes 3:13 (NIV)**

- <u>Love</u>: Harmonious family relationships and friendships

> How good and pleasant it is when God's people live together in unity! **Psalm 133:1 (NIV)**

- <u>Sufficiency</u>: Enough material goods to meet their needs and also extend a hand of generosity to the needy.

> The lions may grow weak and hungry, but those who seek the Lord lack no good thing. **Psalm 34:10 (NIV)**

- <u>Security</u>: A community where they feel safe and accepted.

> My people will live in peaceful dwelling places, in secure homes, in undisturbed places of rest. **Isaiah 32:18 (NIV)**

These are the things we should strive for. A person who has these is happy. This level of living offers a depth of happiness that is unimaginable to people wallowing in the envy, strife and insecurity that accompany materialism.

CHAPTER FOUR: PRINCIPLES OF GODLY WEALTH

God has never prohibited any of those who believed in Him from becoming wealthy. There is no verse in the Bible that tells us that God expects us to renounce wealth and take a vow of poverty in order to serve him. To the contrary, many of the prominent characters of the Bible were men of wealth. It was that fact which allowed many of them to do the work that God had called them to do. For example, it was Joseph's success in Egypt that put him in the position to save his whole family from death by starvation. The bible teaches us that God actually gives us riches as a reward for righteousness. The wisdom of God can give us the insight that we need to become rich. As said earlier, money is a tool for influence and God wants the righteous to have influence in their generation. The only problem God ever had with money is the position it occupies in our lives. God wants money in our hands and not in our hearts.

Having settled this, the question is 'How does God prosper His Children?' We all know how Satan prospers those who serve him, but it is less clear how God brings wealth into the hands of those who obey His commandments. It is the lack of this knowledge that has many people going to church regularly, praying and serving faithfully, yet remaining broke year in year out. Before you can begin your quest for Godly prosperity, one thing you must get clearly into your mind is; THE POVERTY OF THE RIGHTEOUS DOES NOT GLORIFY GOD. The purpose of God is not advanced by His people's backwardness. Think about this; because He did not want the nations to think He was weak, God overlooked Israel's rebellion in the wilderness and brought them into the Promised Land. God always wants to be glorified! Your failure and my poverty do not help the world see God is a better way.

> Then the Lord said to Joshua, "Today I have rolled away the reproach of Egypt from you." So the place has been called Gilgal to this day. **Joshua 5:9 (NIV)**

The above scripture makes it clear to us that God views slavery and everything that accompanies it is as a reproach to His people and a smear on His name. When Israel entered Canaan, He told them that He had rolled away their shame because they were no longer a nameless and powerless people. They now had land, wealth and identity. All of which had been missing in their experience in Egypt. As slaves in Egypt they were insignificant; they did not possess enough power to be an economic force. They were not an important electorate or a group with a respectable culture. They were inconsequential. In the Bible, the greatness of a nation's gods was reflected in the importance of the people. So, if Israel was poor and enslaved, their God was also poor. In the minds of the Egyptians, it meant that the Egyptian gods had overcome the Israelite God. This is why God directly targeted the gods of Egypt in the plagues; He wanted to redeem His name and glory.

> On that same night I will pass through Egypt and strike down every firstborn of both people and animals, and I will bring judgment on all the gods of Egypt. I am the Lord. **Exodus 12:12 (NIV)**

> I will harden the hearts of the Egyptians so that they will go in after them. And I will gain glory through Pharaoh and all his army, through his chariots and his horsemen. **Exodus 14:17 (NIV)**

> He said, "Praise be to the Lord, who rescued you from the hand of the Egyptians and of Pharaoh, and who rescued the people from the hand of the Egyptians. Now I know that the Lord is greater than all other gods, for he did this to those who had treated Israel arrogantly." **Exodus 18:10-11 (NIV)**

Therefore, you need to recognize that God's desire for your prosperity is not just about getting nice things; it is more about God getting the glory. In the same way that a child's dressing and behavior reflect the parents, the world also sees what we do as a reflection of who God is. The struggle for the control of the earth's riches is the physical manifestation of the contest between God and Satan for domination of the earth. As wicked people gain more and more control over resources, the world is made to reflect the nature of Satan more. We see this in the promotion and legalization of wickedness. Satan can do these things because he controls the treasures of the earth and uses them to exercise influence. God is looking for righteous men and women who will offer themselves as trustworthy vessels to whom He will hand over the wealth of the world and use them as vanguards in the promotion of righteousness.

God's Principles of Wealth

What is the difference between how God gives wealth and how the Devil gives wealth? The wealth of Satan comes through lawlessness. But the wealth of God comes through principles. People in the kingdom of Satan will do anything to get their money. They will cut corners; betray friends or whatever else it takes to reach their goals. They do this because money is their overriding purpose. When a person pursues wealth according to God's word, they must do so according to the principles that God has established. They respect the boundaries that God has set and allow their pursuits to follow process. They do this because their overarching purpose is righteousness. Satan's methods offer quick solutions that bring immediate results. When a person follows the way of the Devil, they make quick money. But God's methods create sustainable wealth that is built up slowly but surely.

The principles of Godly wealth are the foundational understandings that undergird our pursuit of wealth. They are called principles because they are infallible, constant and trustworthy. They are infallible because they always work out the same way. They do not work sometimes and fail other times. They are constant because they are always present everywhere on the earth. As a result of their constancy and infallibility, they can be trusted. God has given us these principles to enable us gain control of our own lives and know what to do to move our lives forward. By identifying, understanding, applying and making ourselves adept in each one of them, we dig the foundations of our prosperity deep into the ground, not just for ourselves but for the future generations.

Using the book of Genesis, we will derive the basic principles for Godly wealth

Principle #1: Purpose

God made this entire beautiful world for Himself, but then He decided to share it with us. There is a reason He made it in the first place and He has a purpose in giving it to humankind. To imagine otherwise is immoral and is no different from what Satan does, which is to attempt to claim a world which he did not create for himself. In order to get the best of the world, we must consider the intention of its creator in our actions. What is the purpose for God giving us wealth?

<u>To meet our needs</u>: God wants all your needs to be adequately met.

> I am the Lord your God, who brought you up out of Egypt. Open wide your mouth and I will fill it. **Psalm 81:10 (NIV)**

<u>To give us an enjoyable life</u>: God is not against moderate enjoyment of legitimate pleasures, but He frowns against a self-indulgent lifestyle.

> When the Lord your God has enlarged your territory as he promised you, and you crave meat and say, "I would like some meat," then you may eat as much of it as you want. **Deuteronomy 12:20 (NIV)**

> Do not join those who drink too much wine or gorge themselves on meat, **Proverbs 23:20 (NIV)**

> Whoever loves pleasure will become poor; whoever loves wine and olive oil will never be rich. **Proverbs 21:17 (NIV)**

<u>To help the needy</u>: We are agents of God's grace in the world. His generosity and mercy are extended through our hands. That is one reason He prospers us.

> Do not withhold good from those to whom it is due, when it is in your power to act. Do not say to your neighbor, "Come back tomorrow and I'll give it to you"— when you already have it with you. **Proverbs 3:27-28 (NIV)**

<u>For war</u>: God gives us wealth so that we can have resources to advance just causes.

> This is what the Lord says to his anointed, to Cyrus, whose right hand I take hold of to subdue nations before him and to strip kings of their armor, to open doors before him so that gates will not be shut: I will go before you and will level the mountains; I will break down gates of bronze and cut through bars of iron. I will give you hidden treasures, riches stored in secret places, so that you may know that I am the Lord, the God of Israel, who summons you by name. **Isaiah 45:1-3 (NIV)**

<u>For safekeeping</u>: God gives us wealth so that we can preserve it for the next generation.

> The wise store up choice food and olive oil, but fools gulp theirs down. **Proverbs 21:20 (NIV)**

Principle #2: A Garden and a Seed

In order to create wealth, we need a vessel or an instrument that serves as the channel through which God's blessing flows to us. The blessing is an intangible spiritual element, so it needs a physical instrument to serve as its doorway to enter into the natural world. That physical instrument provides something for the grace of God to rest and act on. Before God can multiply us, we must give Him something to multiply. Too often we wait on God to bless us but there is nothing in our hands to serve as the instrument through which God will bless us. This is very important because the earth exists in a physical realm; therefore everything that God sends to us must make impact on a physical level.

In the book of Genesis, the tangible instruments that God gave to Adam and Eve were a garden and seeds. They were given a physical space where they were to plant seeds and

tend to the plants. That piece of ground became the manifestation of their dominion. The garden represents a job, business or project that you are working at. The seed represents the products of that business, job or project. For example, I may own a bakery. That would be my garden. The seeds of my garden would be the cakes, rolls, burgers and bread that I intend to sell to the public. When I have these, I have provided God a physical basis through which the spiritual virtues that He is releasing into my life will work.

A very important aspect of the seed that we must always remember is that it is always connected to human needs. What gives the products in our garden the ability to become an instrument for blessing is that it can satisfy people's needs. Its ability to meet needs becomes the basis upon which we increase and expand it as the blessing of God increases in our lives. A product that people do not need does not have the ability to create increase.

> You will be blessed in the city and blessed in the country. The fruit of your womb will be blessed, and the crops of your land and the young of your livestock—the calves of your herds and the lambs of your flocks. Your basket and your kneading trough will be blessed. You will be blessed when you come in and blessed when you go out. **Deuteronomy 28:3-6 (NIV)**

> So he went to him and kissed him. When Isaac caught the smell of his clothes, he blessed him and said, "Ah, the smell of my son is like the smell of a field that the Lord has blessed. **Genesis 27:27 (NIV)**

Principle #3: Work

Work is the means by which the spiritual virtue inside us is released into our garden and seed(s). The blessing is already inside us but it needs work to be transformed from a spiritual force into physical results. Work is the proof that you and I believe that God will bless or has blessed us. When a person truly knows that they will succeed, they willingly submit to the process of creating that success. Work is our chance to participate with God in the act of creation. Through work we are not only able to impress our ideas on the world, we also change and remold ourselves. By the use of my hands and mind, I can take a piece of ground and reshape it to fit into a vision in my mind. That vision may be a skyscraper, a lawn or a home. Through work, I take beef and transform it into steak. Whatever the vision is the process by which it is birth into the world is work.

What is work? Anything that creates value, improves the life of the worker, as well as the rest of society. Many people complain that they cannot find work because the type of work that they would rather have is out of their reach. They want a job that carries status and pays a lot of money. Or they just do not want to dirty their hands. People do this because they imagine that their prosperity lies in the job. That is not true; the wealth lies in the person who does the job. A person who has value in them can take something despised by others and make wealth out of it. No matter what you give to a low-quality person, they will always stay broke. In life the ability to handle great things is demonstrated by doing small things well. Secondly, the skills needed to do big things are honed through doing small things. If a person will not work he is denying himself or herself the chance to make wealth.

People who will not work will be barren. They will be unable to birth the dreams they conceive into reality. Many people have been fooled by the message of sweatless success and they are disappointed when pursuing their dream turns out to be a struggle. Some people even believe that since God spoke the world into existence, all they need to create success is to keep a positive mindset and keep speaking affirmative words. But Jesus gives us an idea of how God works when he says, 'the Father works and I also work.' Then he would preach and minister to people all day long, be so tired that He would fall asleep in a violently rocking boat and still wake up before His disciples to go and pray. That is how hard He worked! Hard work does not kill; it shapes our minds and builds our character. Good work ethics creates success, opens doors of opportunity, and makes us a blessing to others.

> Diligent hands will rule, but laziness ends in forced labor. **Proverbs 12:24 (NIV)**

> All hard work brings a profit, but mere talk leads only to poverty. **Proverbs 14:23 (NIV)**

> The sluggard says, "There's a lion outside! I'll be killed in the public square!" **Proverbs 22:13 (NIV)**

> The Lord God took the man and put him in the Garden of Eden to work it and take care of it. **Genesis 2:15 (NIV)**

Principle #4: Gifts

Everybody has a unique set of abilities with which they entered this world. Everyone is best suited to a particular role based on the combination of their abilities, interests, experiences, personality and gender. Discovering that thing which sets you apart from the rest of the world will release you into a position of unique advantage. When a person finds a connection between their passion and their purpose, they are almost unstoppable. That is how God created people to function. Women are passionate about children and that passion matches their purpose as mothers. Children are passionately curious and that matches their need to learn. Men are passionate about work and that matches their needs as providers, God always creates passion in a person for their purpose. Doing that makes what would be a difficult task easier and fun.

Your unique place in life will also serve as the instrument by which all other things are drawn to you. In the experience of David, music which was his passion became the means by which he got into the palace of King Saul. Adam was in the garden working on his passion, when God brought Eve along. It was Jacob's skill as a shepherd that God used to rescue him from Laban and bless him. Your gift will draw to you the people and things that you need to become all that God wants you to be. From the outset, God used abilities to differentiate the roles of humans, as well as animals. Finding your unique contribution makes success much easier. It will also bring joy into your work.

> Adah gave birth to Jabal; he was the father of those who live in tents and raise livestock. His brother's name was Jubal; he was the father of all who play stringed instruments and pipes. Zillah also had a son, Tubal-Cain, who forged all kinds of tools out of bronze and iron. **Genesis 4:20-22 (NIV)**

> We have different gifts, according to the grace given to each of us. If your gift is prophesying, then prophesy in accordance with your faith; if it is serving, then serve; if

it is teaching, then teach; if it is to encourage, then give encouragement; if it is giving, then give generously; if it is to lead, do it diligently; if it is to show mercy, do it cheerfully. **Romans 12:6-8 (NIV)**

Principle #5: People

People are important to the fulfillment of any goal. You need other people to work with you because our purposes often have too many dimensions than we are able to manage on our own. Nobody is equally strong in every department of life. If you think you are, it is because you have not yet moved into a situation that will stretch you. People need others to provide what they do not have. God did not create us to be independent lone rangers; our best selves come forth in the midst of others. Rather than independence and dependence, God wants us to build a network of interdependencies; mutually supportive relationships with others.

God recognized that Adam was insufficient on his own, so he gave him a wife. Even a child can bring perspectives about a situation that we never thought of. The fuller our understanding of life, the more equipped we will be to avoid mistakes and achieve success. However, building our network of relationships requires that we cultivate our social skills and learn how to relate with people of all sorts. We cannot limit our work to only those people who are like us. What matters is that they can help us get where we are going faster and easier. We should not be so fixed in our thinking that others are unable to make an impact on our point of view.

> Two are better than one, because they have a good return for their labor: If either of them falls down, one can help the other up. But pity anyone who falls and has no one to

help them up. Also, if two lie down together, they will keep warm. But how can one keep warm alone? Though one may be overpowered, two can defend themselves. A cord of three strands is not quickly broken. **Ecclesiastes 4:9-12 (NIV)**

Do not forsake your friend or a friend of your family, and do not go to your relative's house when disaster strikes you—better a neighbor nearby than a relative far away. **Proverbs 27:10 (NIV)**

Principle #6: Process

Everything in this world is subject to a process and everything has its own unique process. Process often takes time and requires patience. One of the biggest reasons for the eventual failure of once-successful businesses is that the people running them attempted to grow too fast. They wanted too much too soon and were misled into believing that just because they could buy something, they could also manage it. This is not always true. When we are working at success, there are three kinds of processes that we will have to deal with

Our Personal Development: This deals with your own level of expertise. You cannot operate beyond your level of knowledge and personal growth. Failure will result if you try to do more than you are equipped to do. The only way to accelerate your results is to speed up your learning and growth, rather than by cutting corners.

The Processes within Your Seed: Every seed takes time to germinate, grow and begin to yield fruit. The same is true of a business idea; it must be allowed to grow organically. If you demand the performance of a tree from a sapling, you will destroy it. Bearing in mind that the business or job

involves people and processes, it will only grow as these also develop.

Environmental Processes: No matter how viable a seed and how hard working or smart a farmer is, their results will always be constrained by the surrounding conditions. The nature of the soil and the seasons of the year limit what a seed and farmer can do. In the same way our environment will place limitations on us that will only change with time.

Our efforts are often not enough to change some of the constraints that we will face. It is at such times that we learn to not fret, but be humble, trust God and be led by Him. Processes exist for our development and protection.

> For there is a proper time and procedure for every matter, though a person may be weighed down by misery. **Ecclesiastes 8:6 (NIV)**
>
> Refrain from anger and turn from wrath; do not fret—it leads only to evil. **Psalm 37:8 (NIV)**
>
> Trust in the Lord with all your heart and lean not on your own understanding; in all your ways submit to him, and he will make your paths straight. **Proverbs 3:5-6 (NIV)**

CHAPTER FIVE: KEYS TO KINGDOM WEALTH

Key #1: The Seasons for Success

> And God said, "Let there be lights in the expanse of the heavens to separate the day from the night. And let them be for signs and for seasons, and for days and years, and let them be lights in the expanse of the heavens to give light upon the earth." And it was so. And God made the two great lights—the greater light to rule the day and the lesser light to rule the night—and the stars. **Genesis 1:14-16 (ESV)**

Opportunities occur when there is a meeting of all the different factors that create the conditions for success. Opportunity is a favorable environment for a positive outcome. It is the most powerful natural law for securing the cooperation of the universe in the making of your success. Seasons bring together all the elements that a seed needs to thrive. A seed that decides to bear fruit in its season is certain to have access to all that it needs to succeed within its environment. During the season for a thing, the whole of the world is conspiring to make sure that it wins. Rather than feel resistance, the seed experiences cooperation when it is operating within its season. Seasons make success easier and that is why the natural world depends on the law of seasons in order to avoid struggle.

> As long as the earth endures, seedtime and harvest, cold and heat, summer and winter, day and night will never cease. **Genesis 8:22 (NIV)**

Just as there are seasons for planting and harvesting, there are also seasons for everything people do. The number one cause for poverty is the failure to recognize and take advantage of the seasons of our lives. Young people fail to recognize that the strength of youth is for the purpose of building a secure future for their retirement. You probably know somebody who made a lot of money at a stage in their lives but is broke today because they failed to use that money properly. There are many single people who should have been happily married today but are not because they failed to use the best part of their youth. There are people who are trying to improve themselves and failing at it because they did not do it when they were single and did not have children to feed. Just as trees have season, humans also have periods in their lives most suitable for obtaining success.

> Go to the ant, you sluggard; consider its ways and be wise! It has no commander, no overseer or ruler, yet it stores its provisions in summer and gathers its food at harvest.
> **Proverbs 6:6-8 (NIV)**

The ability to discover and act in the right season has the potential of cutting the effort required for success by more than half. When we discover the season for an endeavor or desire, the whole world will seem to be offering us help. An action carried out in its season appears like an answer to the questions people are asking at that moment. So, there is receptiveness and ease of success. This is very true of the ideas that we pursue in business. An idea that is a response to the conditions of its environment succeeds. The season of success is that time when the environment is demanding the answers that you have. A person trying to sell umbrellas in summer will be frustrated because people are not asking questions about how to be protected from the rain. The problem is not the idea but the season of its launch.

The plant has no control over the season, but only over its ability to be ready for the season. Similarly, you and I have no control over the season. We only have control over our ability to identify and prepare for the season. Have you ever heard the saying that there is no stopping an idea whose time has come? That is because that idea taps into the trends, needs and questions that are engaging the minds of people. It is happening in its season. If you and I must succeed, we must learn to discover the questions that people are asking. We must be sensitive to tap into the discussions that are forefront in the minds of people and take advantage of them. Millionaires are made every day from people observing that a specific thing is gaining in popularity and acting decisively on that insight.

Characteristics of Seasons

- <u>Seasons demand speed</u>. Seasons do not wait and they hardly announce themselves. The change from winter to spring happens seamlessly. The only reason we notice it is because we have experienced it countless times.

- <u>Seasons demand insight</u>. We must be sensitive to the unseen changes in our environment. That means that we must take interest in the people and the issues in our environment.

- <u>Seasons demand action</u>. They do not just demand action, they demand decisive action because seasons do not linger. Therefore in order to take full advantage of them, we must give it our all.

- <u>Seasons demand exertion</u>. A period of extreme hard work, sometimes to the point of exhaustion, is required to take full advantage of the benefits in a season. But once the season passes, there will be a lull and we can rest.

- <u>Seasons demand systematic action</u>. One person acting alone will never be able to take full advantage of a trend. By working with others and finding ways to multiply their impact, they will get a better result. Picture a fisherman casting a fishing line versus a team using nets. Who will enclose the shoal?

> He who gathers crops in summer is a prudent son, but he who sleeps during harvest is a disgraceful son. **Proverbs 10:5 (NIV)**

God has given us seasons as windows of opportunity to obtain our desired result. It allows the farmer to predict and plan his labor because he knows that the difficult times will pass and the favorable times will soon arrive. Seasons create hope and teach patience. Seasons also teach us to be diligent and watchful because they are temporary and if we do not make haste, we will have to wait another year. Without seasons, there would be no need to watch the time and we would never know that our days pass us by. Seasons give us a point of reference to measure the passage of years and apply wisdom to our lives. The knowledge that the favorable conditions will soon pass forces us to work hard. The realization that this year's harvest is all we have until next year's, teaches us to manage our resources. Seasons are blessing to the diligent and a curse to the indolent.

Key #2: Seedtime and Harvest

> If clouds are full of water, they pour rain on the earth. Whether a tree falls to the south or to the north, in the place where it falls, there it will lie. Ecclesiastes 11:3 (NIV)

The verse above teaches us that some things are the inevitable consequences of some other things. It also explains that there are situations which depend on specific actions from people before they can change. Rainfall is the inevitable result of the clouds overflowing with water. This means that if the clouds have not been filled with water previously, there will not be rain. Therefore, the key that unlocks rain in our lives is the presence of clouds. The action that we must take with the cloud is to fill it with water. The verse further tells us that obstacles are never removed except an external force is applied to them. When a tree falls, the force of gravity can pull it in any direction. If you do not like the place where the tree lies, you have to apply a force of your own to move it. Otherwise the tree remains there. You cannot trust the forces in nature to arrange the tree exactly the way you would want it.

This scripture teaches us the necessity of making connections in order to understand the outcomes that we are experiencing or observing. If we do not see the link between the fullness of the clouds and rain falling on us, we will never find the point where we should focus action. Therefore, the key to changing our lives and taking charge of our future is to understand the processes at work in our environment. Having understood those processes, we must find a point of entry, from which we can participate and influence the outcomes. If we do not do this, we will be at the mercy of whatever fills our clouds with water. We will never have rain in our lives when we want it; a life without control and power. By understanding the relationship between the cause and the effect, we can become proactive and start to move the fallen trees of our lives out of the way to create a path for our success.

> Sluggards do not plow in season; so at harvest time they look but find nothing. **Proverbs 20:4 (NIV)**
>
> He who gathers crops in summer is a prudent son, but he who sleeps during harvest is a disgraceful son. **Proverbs 10:5 (NIV)**

Just as what causes a baby is a pregnancy, what causes a harvest is planting a seed. The harvest is the natural outcome of putting something into the ground and nurturing it to maturity. The harvest we see today is the end of a process which began sometime in somebody's past. Today's success is the fruit of yesterday's labor. Whatever you are experiencing today is the yield of the actions and inactions of the past - yours and others. In order to experience a particular result, you must discover the exact seed - action - that creates it, and then plant that seed or act on that knowledge. This is true for things we want to see in our finances, relationships or health. Everything that we are today is an effect which began as a cause. People never think about the seeds, they just expect the results. That is like not lighting the fire and wondering why you are cold. Every success is conceived and birth through the pregnancy of intentional actions.

> Do not be deceived: God cannot be mocked. A man reaps what he sows. Whoever sows to please their flesh, from the flesh will reap destruction; whoever sows to please the Spirit, from the Spirit will reap eternal life.
> **Galatians 6:7-8 (NIV)**

This truth is what is often referred to as the law of harvest. It highlights the power of the choices that people make. It teaches us that the decisions and actions of our lives are not without consequences. Rather they start a chain reaction of events that often result in totally unexpected outcomes. The only control we have over the outcome is the action. If we do not take the action, we have ensured that the outcome will not happen because we have eliminated the chance of it happening. This law is true for both negative and positive actions. The good deeds we do kick-start a sequence of events that result in good things coming into our lives. The law of harvests is neutral; it neither bad nor good. It gives each person the power to frame the world they want to live in by giving them the seeds for creating that world, their actions. There are seven laws or dimensions to the law of harvest.

Law #1: We Must Plant Something To Harvest Something

Without taking action, we should not expect results. If you want to see something in your life, go out there and do it. If the seed of action is not planted, the harvest of reward should not be expected. Emptiness multiplied over a thousand times will still produce emptiness. There has to be an action before there can be a reaction.

> All hard work brings a profit, but mere talk leads only to poverty. **Proverbs 14:23 (NIV)**

Law #2: We Reap The Same As What We Sowed

You cannot gather good fruit from a bad tree because a seed always produces according to what it carries inside it. Therefore, a seed of good deeds carries within it good deeds and will yield a harvest of good deeds to the person who planted it. If you plant hatred, you will also reap the same. If you plant diligence, you will reap prosperity. But laziness will produce plenty of hunger.

> By their fruit you will recognize them. Do people pick grapes from thorn-bushes, or figs from thistles? **Matthew 7:16 (NIV)**

> Those who work their land will have abundant food, but those who chase fantasies have no sense. **Proverbs 12:11 (NIV)**

Law #3: Our Harvest Does Not Come In The Season We Planted

The results of our actions are not always immediately evident but they are always inevitable. Sometimes people attempt to achieve a goal and after applying themselves to it for a period, they give up because they did not see the expected results. This is because they failed to understand there is always a period of incubation between when we plant our seed and when we harvest it. This is why we not only have to be patient in waiting for the harvest; we also have to keep sowing the good seeds to create more harvest.

> Let us not become weary in doing good, for at the proper time we will reap a harvest if we do not give up. **Galatians 6:9 (NIV)**

> Be patient, then, brothers and sisters... See how the farmer waits for the land to yield its valuable crop, patiently waiting for the autumn and spring rains. You too, be patient and stand firm... **James 5:7-8 (NIV)**

Law #4: We Receive Back More Than We Planted

We reap the results of our actions multiplied many times over. The consequences and results do not come to us in the same measure as the action. In the same way that a farmer puts one apple seed into the ground to get a tree full of apples, or an investor puts up a hundred dollars to receive a thousand, our deeds also come back to us multiplied.

> They sow the wind and reap the whirlwind. **Hosea 8:7 (NIV)**

> Isaac planted crops in that land and the same year reaped a hundredfold, because the Lord blessed him. **Genesis 26:12 (NIV)**

Law #5: Our Harvest Is In Proportion To What We Sow

The returns we get depend on the level of investment we made. A person who plants on an acre will get less than someone who plants on two acres. The seeds they both planted will multiply. But if the first person has one hundred seeds multiplying, the second will have two hundred. It is only fair that since he did additional work cultivating extra land and planting more seeds, his harvest should also be greater.

> Remember this: Whoever sows sparingly will also reap sparingly, and whoever sows generously will also reap generously. **2 Corinthians 9:6 (NIV)**

> Give, and it will be given to you. A good measure, pressed down, shaken together and running over, will be poured into your lap. For with the measure you use, it will be measured to you. **Luke 6:38 (NIV)**

Law #6: Good Seeds Need Constant Nurture, Bad Seeds Grow On Their Own

Just like a farmer does not need to do anything to make weeds grow on his farm, in the same way evil deeds will yield a harvest on their own. Good deeds, like the good seeds of the farmer, need to be protected. This means that if we start something good, we have to sustain it by continuing to do more of that same thing, in order to receive the full benefits in time. It takes effort to fly and none at all to fall; that is why birds have to keep flapping their wings.

> It will produce thorns and thistles for you and you will eat the plants of the field. **Genesis 3:18 (NIV)**

> I went past the field of a sluggard, past the vineyard of someone who has no sense; thorns had come up everywhere, the ground was covered with weeds, and the stone wall was in ruins. I applied my heart to what I observed and learned a lesson from what I saw: A little sleep, a little slumber, a little folding of the hands to rest—and poverty will come on you like a thief and scarcity like an armed man. **Proverbs 24:30-34 (NIV)**

Law #7: Do Not Fret About Yesterday's Harvest, Focus on Tomorrow's Sowing

When you become fixated on the current circumstances of your life, you are focusing your energies on last year's harvest, that is, the consequences of past actions. You cannot go back into the past and change the seeds that are producing the negative results that you are experiencing. You can sow good seeds today which will produce positive results for you tomorrow. Rather than be stuck in yesterday, learn from the mistakes of the past and let them guide your actions in making a better future today.

> Brothers and sisters, I do not consider myself yet to have taken hold of it. But one thing I do: Forgetting what is behind and straining toward what is ahead. **Philippians 3:13 (NIV)**

CHAPTER SIX: EVERYTHING BEGINS WITH A SEED

Understanding Your Seeds

What are the seeds that are given to you and I, with which we can change our lives? There are three categories of seeds that we can sow in life; seeds of thoughts, seeds of words and seeds of actions. These three categories comprise all of the resources within a person's reach to transform their own lives and affect the experiences of those around them. Everything that you and I contend with and will ever contend with in life began as a thought before it became words and finally materialized in an action. This is also true of whatever God does in the lives of His children; He begins at the level of our thinking, proceeds to the words that we speak and finally manifests them in our actions. God cannot change a person until He can positively influence their thinking, their words and their actions. Until there is harmony between thoughts, words and actions, we will be unable to harness the full potential that is within us to create success.

> For it is with your heart that you believe and are justified, and it is with your mouth that you profess your faith and are saved. **Romans 10:10 (NIV)**

The Seeds of Thoughts

You cannot think wrong and live right. Your thoughts are the hidden source from which your life draws. Everything that your life is today is the result of the hidden notions and beliefs that you hold inside your mind. The way that you see yourself; that is, what you judge yourself capable of doing or not doing are all the fruits of your thoughts. The way that you view people around you and the world in general are functions of your thoughts. The more you think something, the more it becomes real and the greater its potential for directing the course of your life. Your mind is a garden and the thoughts that you think are the seeds that you plant in that garden. When those thoughts have taken root and become fully grown, they will manifest themselves as actions. You cannot think one thing and do another thing. Your life goes in the direction of your thoughts.

> Above all else, guard your heart, for everything you do flows from it. **Proverbs 4:23 (NIV)**

> You brood of vipers, how can you who are evil say anything good? For the mouth speaks what the heart is full of. A good man brings good things out of the good stored up in him, and an evil man brings evil things out of the evil stored up in him. **Matthew 12:34-35 (NIV)**

The following quote from an 1856 newspaper in Colchester, England illustrates the point 'Mr. Wiseman then cautioned his young friends as to the habits they contracted in early life:—"Whatsoever a man soweth that shall he also reap." You sow an act, you reap a habit (acts repeated constitute habits); you sow a habit, you reap a character; you sow a character, you reap a destiny. Let them, he said, cultivate habits of industry, application, and order, and they might rely upon it, with God's blessing, they would succeed in life." What we think consistently will dominate us. Many people try to change their lives by focusing only on changing their behavior and relationships. They fail to recognize that lifestyles and relationships are creations of thoughts and beliefs. To change your life, begin with your thoughts.

> Finally, brothers and sisters, whatever is true, whatever is noble, whatever is right, whatever is pure, whatever is lovely, whatever is admirable—if anything is excellent or praiseworthy—think about such things.
> **Philippians 4:8 (NIV)**

In order to change your thoughts, you must watch the things that feed your thoughts. If you keep watching negative things on television and the internet, those will be the things that dominate your life. In order to uproot the tree of hate, anger, fear, self-doubt, laziness, lust and other wrong behavior you indulge in, you must stop watering them. Every thought that you think has an origin; it was created by someone telling it to you or by an experience. That thought becomes a reality as it is confirmed and sustained by things in your environment. In order to deal with the thought, you must cut off its life support; those things which give it power. These include people, places and activities that reinforce the thought. Separate yourself from such things, if you want to own your mind and control your life.

The Seeds of Words

Words are a potent force and they create our world. Think about it, so much of the things that we take for granted are built on words. When the president is sworn in, the ceremony is based on words. We judge the success and failure of the administration on the basis of their campaign promises, words. The glue that keeps our economies running is words; agreements and contracts between millions of different organizations, some of whose leaders have never met or spoken to each other. On a more personal level, words have determined which people have entered, stayed in or left your life. When you think of relationships that did not work out, many of them failed because of wrong words that

were spoken or right words that were not spoken. Words are so powerful that they keep our world working, yet they are the most misused things in life because everyone has them.

> Words from the mouth of the wise are gracious, but fools are consumed by their own lips. **Ecclesiastes 10:12 (NIV)**

> The tongue also is a fire, a world of evil among the parts of the body. It corrupts the whole body, sets the whole course of one's life on fire, and is itself set on fire by hell. **James 3:6 (NIV)**

> For by your words you will be acquitted, and by your words you will be condemned. **Matthew 12:37 (NIV)**

These verses are saying that people can create hell on earth for themselves by the words that they speak. In other words, your own words can set your whole world on fire. This is why the wise know how to use words carefully. They realize that words are a force that moves. They can move the hearers to anger or laughter, to hate or love, to fear or faith. Words determine whether we are opening our own paths or impeding our own progress. They determine if people respond to us with favor or react with anger. Words have the ability to stir up rage and quell hatred. A person who uses words well will reduce or even remove their need to ever use the sword because they can keep conflicts from escalating into violence. The right use of words can save a person from injury and prevent them from wasting valuable time in needless squabbles. If we know how to use words we can open a pathway through hard rock.

> One who loves a pure heart and who speaks with grace will have the king for a friend. **Proverbs 22:11 (NIV)**

> Kings take pleasure in honest lips; they value the one who speaks what is right. **Proverbs 16:13 (NIV)**

Words also determine the quality of people that we can relate to. Most people can only communicate at the level of the environment they live in. As a result, they are limited to results within that environment. If a person can only speak street language, he will find it hard to fit into an organized corporate setting. However, even if a person lives in the ghetto and knows how to communicate in the language of business people, he may be given a chance. Many successful businesses remain small because their owners cannot speak the language of finance. Therefore, they are unable to get bank loans or attract investors. The words you use can shut or open doors of opportunities because words are your calling card. It does not matter how well you dress, people's impressions about you are formed by what comes out when you open your mouth.

> We all stumble in many ways. Anyone who is never at fault in what they say is perfect, able to keep their whole body in check. **James 3:2 (NIV)**

> Even fools are thought wise if they keep silent, and discerning if they hold their tongues. **Proverbs 17:28 (NIV)**

Seeds of Actions

> All hard work brings a profit, but mere talk leads only to poverty. **Proverbs 14:23 (NIV)**

Action is what takes thoughts and words and give them power. When thoughts and words do not create actions, it leads to unfruitfulness. Whatever results we want to see in our lives today, must be created in the actions that we are taking today. The amount of love that you have in your life is the result of the amount of love that you have given. The amount of money you have today is the consequence of what you did with the money you had in the past. The amount of spiritual favor you enjoy is the fruit of the spiritual actions that you have taken in the past. Without an action in the past, success cannot be created in the future. Actions are the levers by which we turn our destinies. Actions give us something to which we can apply our knowledge and faith; without those we will be operating in a vacuum.

> What good is it, my brothers and sisters, if someone claims to have faith but has no deeds? Can such faith save them? ...faith by itself, if it is not accompanied by action, is dead. As the body without the spirit is dead, so faith without deeds is dead. **James 2:14/17/26 (NIV)**

The chief reason many people do not have any money is that they do not take positive actions to make their dreams a reality. This could be due to their being too lazy or too scared to take action. They fail to realize that the hardest part of any endeavor is starting it. Getting ourselves out of a comfortable place is the most difficult thing to do. Fear of failing will fill the mind with paralyzing thoughts that cripple our ability to make any move. Sometimes the excuses may even be legitimate; it may be true that you do not have any education or money. Until you try and give your best, you do not know that those excuses can actually prevent you from succeeding. Most times the difficulties that prevent people from succeeding are more imagined than they are real. Laziness and fear amplify difficulties. If you take a

step, you will discover that the trouble has been grossly overrated.

> The slothful man says, "There is a lion in the way! A lion is in the streets!" Proverbs 26:13 (MEV)

A person who hates work despises success. There is no easy way to get wealth. The irony is that what people call the easy way is often harder than the so-called hard way. The dishonest and immoral person does not realize that they cannot escape working hard; they simply divert the hard work to other areas of their lives. The liar works hard to remember all the lies they told and to whom they told each one. The prostitute works hard to escape the shame and guilt of her lifestyle. The conman works hard to shut the voice of his conscience. There is no easy road to success. The difference between the person who works hard and the one who is dishonest is when they choose to gain their rewards. The honest person chooses to struggle today to enjoy tomorrow. But the dishonest person wants to enjoy now and therefore has to suffer later.

> Good understanding gives favor, but the way of transgressors is hard. **Proverbs 13:15 (MEV)**

> Stern discipline awaits anyone who leaves the path; the one who hates correction will die. **Proverbs 15:10 (NIV)**

Seeds of Giving

When somebody takes a job, what they have done is contracted to exchange their energy, time and skill for some of the employer's material resources. At the end of each day, week or month, they are paid an amount of money. That money is the equivalent of the value of the work they have done. Their energy and skills are quantified in terms of money. In the same way, when a farmer harvests his crops, he will exchange them for money. The amount of money he gets is an indication of the value that people place on his skills and effort. Of course, this value is not always an accurate measure of a person's contribution to the society. Since money is a creation of human beings, it is bound to be imperfect like human beings. However, what is important to understand is that when people exchange money, they are actually trading in personal worth.

This is why when a farmer gives some of the money he earned from his crops to another person; he is actually giving them some of his crops. Taken further, he is giving them some of the effort and skills he invested to grow those crops. Taken even further, he is giving them a part of his life, since life is made up of time and time is what he has invested in creating that harvest. This is why many people find it hard to part with their money. They feel that asking them to give money is like taking a part of themselves. This feeling is natural, since they literally gave a part of themselves to make that money. This is why one of the most important ways to demonstrate value for anything is to invest money in it. This may be a person you love, or a cause you value or some knowledge you want, you demonstrate your value for it by giving money to it.

> Again, the kingdom of heaven is like a merchant looking for fine pearls. When he found one of great value, he went away and sold everything he had and bought it. **Matthew 13:45-46 (NIV)**

This is why money is a seed; which we only give to things that we want to own or grow. If we want to build a relationship, we invest our money in it. That relationship may be with someone at the same level as us, like a friend or a spouse. It may be someone lower than us, like a child or a needy person. Or it may be someone above us, such as a mentor or God. Giving to a relationship is like watering a plant to make it grow. Sometimes, however, people do not see the need for giving to those who are ahead of them. We feel that they have more than enough and may not even value our gifts. Yet we see no problem in giving to someone we are in love with, even if they do not need the gift. We know that giving is a way to communicate the value we place on the relationship. The exact same logic applies to giving to those who are above us.

> When Jesus heard this, he said to him, "You still lack one thing. Sell everything you have and give to the poor, and you will have treasure in heaven. Then come, follow me."
> **Luke 18:22 (NIV)**

This leads us to a valuable principle which anyone seeking Godly wealth must understand; the principle of exchange. There must always be an exchange of something valuable for every spiritual endowment. The blessings of God are valuable and we have to demonstrate the value we place on them. Everyone wants to get the gifts of God but not everyone values the gifts enough to pay for them. The way to prove that we value God's blessings is to also give something we treasure to Him. Jesus always demanded that those who wanted to become his disciples gave up something to prove the value they had for what He offered. They did not do this to meet God's need but to demonstrate their commitment. This spiritual principle is often lost to people in the modern age, because we expect that everything should be given to us for free. This principle has not changed and will be discussed further in the next chapter.

> Do not give dogs what is sacred; do not throw your pearls to pigs. If you do, they

may trample them under their feet, and turn and tear you to pieces. **Matthew 7:6 (NIV)**

Finding The Right Field

There is one thing which is more important than the seed. That is the environment in which a seed is planted. That environment determines if the seed will struggle or thrive. Every plant has a perfect soil in which it will flourish. Peanuts need sandy soil that is dry. Swamp rice needs waterlogged clay soils. If you put peanuts in the rice environment, they will not succeed. As a matter of fact, they will die, but if they manage to survive, they will not produce any seeds. Where you put your seeds matter, it is not enough to have seeds. People are regularly planting seeds of thoughts, words, actions and money, without getting the harvests that they are looking for. This is usually because they are planting the wrong seeds or planting the right seeds in the wrong place or at the wrong time.

The word of God teaches us that there are four categories of places where we should sow our seeds. We can sow seeds into our relationships, our finances, charitable deeds and the Kingdom of God.

Field# 1: Relationships

> Two are better than one, because they have a good return for their labor: If either of them falls down, one can help the other up. But pity anyone who falls and has no one to help them up. Also, if two lie down together, they will keep warm. But how can one keep warm alone? Though one may be overpowered, two can defend themselves. A cord of three strands is not quickly broken. **Ecclesiastes 4:9-12 (NIV)**

Relationships create the ecosystems necessary for our success. When we think of relationships in connection to wealth building, we immediately think of business relationships. The family is the most important relationship for building prosperity. This is because the family serves as our most important support system. The family validates us as someone worthy of success, strengthens us in times of weakness and its collective insights help to guide us. By investing good words, time and money into making our families strong, we are building strong foundations underneath us to carry whatever dreams and visions we conceive. The more whole our family, the more positive energy we can draw from it to put into our endeavors. Not building the family while chasing wealth is like pouring water into a basket.

In addition to our families, we must cultivate other relationships. Positive relationships serve as sources of opportunity, information and support; the more of them we have, the greater the probability of success. A large network of valuable relationships makes it easier to prosper because there is always someone who has what you need to move forward or knows someone who does. This is why the best jobs are gotten by referrals. It is also the reason why some ethnic groups are able to succeed more than others. They have learned to build networks for mutual support and as a result can multiply and sustain their wealth over long periods of time. It is easier to become wealthy when you have a community of people supporting your aspirations.

> As iron sharpens iron, so one person sharpens another. **Proverbs 27:17 (NIV)**

This is why it is very important to invest time, energy and money into affirmative relationships. Everything that God created is incomplete; it needs something else in order to succeed. Plants need the soil, fish need water, and animals need grass. God created everything to be interdependent. He does not have a problem with people depending on others; He has a problem with people being parasites. You must cultivate self-sufficiency in those things that you can do for yourself, while cultivating relationships for those things you cannot do. By learning from and working with others, you can work with the hands of many rather than yours alone. Nurture your personal, professional, business and community relationships. Do not underestimate people, because you never know who they know or who they may become

Field #2: Your Own Business

> The little you had before I came has increased greatly, and the Lord has blessed you wherever I have been. But now, when may I do something for my own household?
> **Genesis 30:30 (NIV)**

One of the biggest reasons for poverty today is people sowing good seed in other people's fields. Most people do not know where their field is; they mistake someone else's field for their own. Working at a job and earning a salary is not the same as sowing in your own field. Just as working on a farm does not make you the owner of it. The person who owns the land and the seeds planted in it is the owner of the farm. Even if the owner hires an overseer to manage the farm, it is still the owner's property. The overseer may work on the farm like it was his own and may even make it more fruitful than the owner could, yet in the end, he must surrender the harvest to the owner of the field. Just because you work in a place and occupy a position of authority or contribute a lot of value, it does not make that place your field.

What makes a place your field is that you have control over it, have a share of the profits from it and will continue to enjoy those benefits even if you do not work there every day. If you are paid wages or a salary, you are not the owner but a hired hand. A hired hand does not have a secure future, the owner does. It is alright to work at a job as long as it advances your goal of getting something that belongs to you. Far too many people do not understand this; they mistakenly think that if they treat the job well, they will be treated right by the company. Sadly, most people find out too late that this is not always true. If you have no say in the overall direction of a business, do not share in its profits and cannot leave it to your children, it does not belong to you. It is a disservice to yourself to build for others what you do not have yourself.

> Anyone who does not provide for their relatives, and especially for their own household, has denied the faith and is worse than an unbeliever. **1 Timothy 5:8 (NIV)**

Field #3: Charitable Deeds

> Whoever shuts their ears to the cry of the poor will also cry out and not be answered. **Proverbs 21:13 (NIV)**

> The generous will themselves be blessed, for they share their food with the poor. **Proverbs 22:9 (NIV)**

A person who gives to the poor helps themselves. They do this by assisting the poor to rise out of poverty. Doing so builds a wall of protection around his wealth because his generosity has prevented that poor person from becoming a thief who will break into his property. By helping others, you make it possible for them to also get for themselves what you have gotten. This allows you to enjoy your suc-

cess better. The reason most rich people live behind fortresses is fear; they know that the poor are looking for the chance to tear that wealth out of their hands. A generous man secures more peace of mind for himself by removing the desperation that drives people into crime. By giving to others, they sow seeds of hope and encourage people to keep trying to be better. A rich man who does not help others does not understand the purpose of wealth.

> Those who give to the poor will lack nothing, but those who close their eyes to them receive many curses. **Proverbs 28:27 (NIV)**

Additionally, generosity to those who are in need builds a store of goodwill for the giver. The people who benefit from your goodness will hold you in high esteem and also tell others about your deeds. That person is building a store of blessings for their children in the future. The rewards of their gifts outlive them because the children of those poor people will remember the good things that were done for their parents. Our generosity builds goodwill and goodwill is a valuable asset, regardless of what wealth a person has today. By helping the poor, we build safety nets for ourselves in the day of misfortune. The poor person we help today may become the means for our salvation tomorrow. This is true because nobody has custody of tomorrow and we cannot predict what may happen to us or our success.

Field #4: God's Kingdom

> This is what the Lord Almighty says: "Give careful thought to your ways. Go up into the mountains and bring down timber and build my house, so that I may take pleasure in it and be honored," says the Lord. "You expected much, but see, it turned out to be little. What you brought home, I blew away.

Why?" declares the Lord Almighty. "Because of my house, which remains a ruin, while each of you is busy with your own house. Therefore, because of you the heavens have withheld their dew and the earth its crops. I called for a drought on the fields and the mountains, on the grain, the new wine, the olive oil and everything else the ground produces, on people and livestock, and on all the labor of your hands." **Haggai 1:7-11 (NIV)**

All wealth has a purpose and serves something. Although money has no character in itself, since it is just paper or metal, it still possesses character. It assumes the character of the person who owns it. A person's wealth flows in the direction of their love and desire - those things that they invest money in. If you examine what a nation spends the most money on and who it pays the most, you get an indication of the things its government and citizens value the most. What we hate we starve of money, but what we love we provide with money. We never have money for things we do not care about, yet we cannot seem to spend enough money on the things that we love. If people are not giving their money to something they claim to love, they really do not love it. Money is an instrument for holding up the things that matter to us.

Money is a tool and a weapon for establishing ideas. Your money either serves darkness or God. Money is never neutral because the people who own money are not neutral. Believers may indirectly be financing the enemies of God by the things they spend their money on. What you regularly give money to becomes the greatest influence in your society. People will not balk at paying hundreds of dollars for a sporting event, but gripe over putting ten dollars in a church offering. They will ask for explanations about what

the money is for. Yet they never ask what the sporting event really does for them. At the end of the day, these same people wonder why there is no voice to speak against unrighteousness in their society. They conveniently forget how they starved the church out of the money it needed to fulfill its purpose.

CHAPTER SEVEN: DIVINE BLUEPRINT FOR WEALTH; GOD'S PART

> But blessed is the one who trusts in the Lord, whose confidence is in him. They will be like a tree planted by the water that sends out its roots by the stream. It does not fear when heat comes; its leaves are always green. It has no worries in a year of drought and never fails to bear fruit. **Jeremiah 17:7-8 (NIV)**

A person or group's ability to influence the events that happen around them is directly connected to the extent to which they control resources. This is why God prioritizes the prosperity of His children. Every form of spiritual power must eventually manifest itself as a material power in order to make an impact in the world. If the church claims to have spiritual authority, it must be evident in our prosperity and influence. The acquisition of spiritual power is always matched by the acquisition of material power. The more powerful an idea, the more people, land and money it controls. This is why the United States is considered the most powerful nation on the earth; its ideas control much of the world and consequently it directs major portions of world resources. The same can be said of Islam in the Middle-East and China in Asia.

This is why every time God begins to set up a man or a nation, He arms them with wealth. God acknowledges wealth as the physical evidence of spiritual power. When He gave Adam and Eve spiritual authority over the earth; He gave them real estate as the proof of it. When God elevated Abraham as the messenger of His covenant, He gave him wealth. Actually, the more Abraham understood and followed God's plans, the more wealth and influence he acquired. Also, God could use Joseph as his instrument to de-

liver His children because Joseph had political influence and control of enormous wealth. Finally, when God delivered the children of Israel from slavery, He arranged for them to gain the wealth of Egypt. He knew that in order for them to be a force, they had to have material power.

> Abram had become very wealthy in livestock and in silver and gold. **Genesis 13:2 (NIV)**

God does not have a problem with money; He has a problem with what money does to people. The issue that God has with money is that people tend to serve money. We fail to understand money as a tool for fulfilling purpose and make it the reason for our existence. It is this misplacement of values that leads God to ask people to give up money. The process of surrendering wealth allows money to lose its hold on our hearts. This is why Jesus said that after we have given it up, we would gain it back a hundredfold. In other words, God would give us more money than we had or ever imagined we could have when He becomes sure that our hearts are in the right place. It is important to understand that when Jesus asked people to give up their wealth, what He was taking away was their materialism and not their money.

> Truly I tell you, Jesus replied, no one who has left home or brothers or sisters or mother or father or children or fields for me and the gospel will fail to receive a hundred times as much in this present age: homes, brothers, sisters, mothers, children and fields—along with persecutions—and in the age to come eternal life. **Mark 10:29-30 (NIV)**

God's Promise To Prosper Us

> The lions may grow weak and hungry, but those who seek the Lord lack no good thing. **Psalm 34:10 (NIV)**

> For the Lord God is a sun and shield; the Lord bestows favor and honor; no good thing does he withhold from those whose walk is blameless. **Psalm 84:11 (NIV)**

God always anchors His invitation to people on the promise of a better life. He said to Abraham 'I will bless you and make your name great.' He said to the children of Israel 'I will give you a land flowing with milk and honey.' He also said to them 'if you heed me, you will eat the finest of wheat.' In the New Testament, Jesus said 'I have come that they may have life abundantly.' God has always made it clear to people that His intention for their lives is to make them better than they used to be. That is why when Abraham followed God, he rose out of poverty, obscurity and infertility. When the children of Israel followed God, they emerged from slavery into a strong nation. If we follow God, there is also a promise of blessings awaiting us.

> The thief comes only to steal and kill and destroy; I have come that they may have life, and have it to the full. **John 10:10 (NIV)**

Yet, although He wants to release all the treasures of wealth that belong to Him into the hands of His children, everything He wants to do with us and for us depends on our agreement with Him. Our lives must be lived according to the higher goals that He sets before us. The whole earth was created by God and is owned by Him. The Devil and all the people who serve him take what God has created and use them in ways that God never intended. If we are also going to take God's blessings and misuse them, then there is no point in Him giving them to us. God is not going to give us His resources only for us to use them against Him. He already has more than enough demons and humans doing that. The gifts and blessings of God are reserved for His loyal servants, not rebels. How do we demonstrate our loyalty to God?

> But remember the Lord your God, for it is he who gives you the ability to produce wealth, and so confirms his covenant, which he swore to your ancestors, as it is today. **Deuteronomy 8:18 (NIV)**

If you look at the verse quoted above, you will see that it has many significant components. First, it declares that our prosperity comes from God. Then it says that the method God uses to bring wealth into our lives is by giving us power. Additionally, it states that the reason God does all of this is to establish His covenant. And finally, it admonishes us to remember the Lord. The summary; there are two parts to God's wealth plan for his children. There is the part that is God's responsibility and another part that is man's responsibility. God puts within our reach all the natural, human and spiritual resources that we need to succeed. Our part is to understand and follow His guidelines in terms of our worship, work, possessions, and relationships.

God's Part: The Blessing

> The blessing of the Lord brings wealth, without painful toil for it. **Proverbs 10:22 (NIV)**

When God blesses something, it is a command for that thing to thrive. God's blessing is a pronouncement that releases the spiritual forces that bring together whatever that thing needs to flourish. God's blessing will steer us to the right places, causing the right people to cross our paths and the wrong ones to leave our lives. It will make people who have the things we need to favor us. It will protect us from pain and loss. It will create happiness. Blessedness is different from wealth. People can have wealth without being blessed. A blessed person has their lives divinely ordered for positive things. The blessing of God on our bodies causes fruitfulness. It will make our children strong and healthy. The blessing of God on our work causes us to get much from it than we put in - hundredfold return instead of thirtyfold.

Everything that God gives us in order to make us prosper can be summed up as 'The Blessing.' The actions of the blessing working within our lives is what creates 'the power to get wealth'

An Enlightened Mind

> Evildoers do not understand what is right, but those who seek the Lord understand it fully. Proverbs **28:5 (NIV)**

> I have more understanding than the elders, for I obey your precepts. **Psalm 119:100 (NIV)**

This is the ability to fully understand the outcome of an action before we undertake it. The person whose mind has been blessed in this way is able to discern the right course of action because he can see the ultimate end of the various options that lie open to him. Therefore he is able to choose those paths that consistently bring lasting outcomes. With the result that his life is a steady upward climb. He is not experiencing the 'up and downs' of the wicked who cannot see the outcome of their choices but constantly choose the shortest route.

A person who has an enlightened mind will be energized in his mind to see beyond what most people can. He can make connections, identify trends and understand human behavior. Here are a few things that begin to happen to someone who diligently applies the blessing that God has deposited in their mind;

- They realize that paying people well makes them more money in the long run than they would have saved in the short run by cheating them. They realize that the cost micromanaging unhappy staff, reworking goods and hiring new people is not worth the trouble.

- They will have a grand view of their environment and be able to understand the underlying forces beneath the events people see. That way they are able to sense things before they happen, and position for that eventuality.

- They will become skillful at their work and be able to develop and deploy the best processes and systems for creating goods and services more efficiently.

- They will gain the insight from the word of God on how to manage a large enterprise comprising of disparate parts and numerous people; making them all work in unison. They will become expert administrators.

- They will be able to draw up systems and programs that also guarantee a future for those who work for them; because they recognize that by giving others a future they give themselves stability.

- They will learn how to attract and maintain relationships with the great because they understand their needs in a way others do not. They will serve great men; kings and nobles, and in so doing become great themselves.

All these were the characteristics of Joseph, which enabled him to set himself apart from the rest of the slaves and staff in the house of Potiphar. The blessing gave him an edge that others could only describe as a 'magic touch.' We also see the same process at work in the life of Daniel, who although he was a slave and eunuch, rose to the post of Prime Minister in the Persian Kingdom. Daniel was so phenomenal, that he served three Emperors.

> God gave Solomon wisdom and very great insight, and a breadth of understanding as measureless as the sand on the seashore. **1 Kings 4:29 (NIV)**

Gifts, Abilities and Inspired Ideas

> And I have filled him with the Spirit of God, with wisdom, with understanding, with knowledge and with all kinds of skills— to make artistic designs for work in gold, silver and bronze, to cut and set stones, to work in wood, and to engage in all kinds of crafts. **Exodus 31:3-5 (NIV)**

Every person in this world has an ability which sets them apart from those around them. This is something God gives us as a trump card in the world. Many people never find their gifts because they think only singers, actors, athletes, public speakers, preachers, etc, have gifts. Your gift can be something as simple as combining colors or seeing the problems in a plan. If you have not discovered your gifts, it is most likely that you have not exposed yourself to situations that allow it to manifest or you have not paid enough attention to yourself. By not knowing what you are good at, you make success much harder. Joseph had an ability to interpret dreams. When he combined his work ethic, integrity, human relationships and spiritual gifts, he experienced

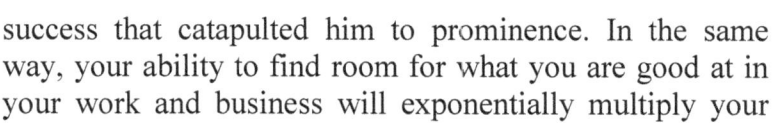

success that catapulted him to prominence. In the same way, your ability to find room for what you are good at in your work and business will exponentially multiply your impact.

> There are different kinds of service, but the same Lord. There are different kinds of working, but in all of them and in everyone it is the same God at work. **1 Corinthians 12:5-6 (NIV)**

God gives people the seed of ideas; a thought for solving a problem or creating a better solution than that which already exists. Inspired ideas are powerful paths to success. The problem is most people do not keep track of their ideas. Your most successful ideas will not arrive in an earth-shattering encounter but often in moments of stillness or through intractable problems. However, if you have not made something of the seemingly insignificant ideas, the big ones will elude you. By valuing the random insights that come into your head and documenting them, you are setting yourself up to receive a great idea in the future. It is no use to have ideas that you do not pursue. As a matter of fact, the big idea will usually come in the course of pursuing the small ideas. Oftentimes it is the failure of the small ideas which lead to the discovery of the big ideas.

> If any of you lacks wisdom, you should ask God, who gives generously to all without finding fault, and it will be given to you. **James 1:5 (NIV)**

God is always poised to deliver solutions to the problems of humanity through inspired ideas, but we have to position ourselves to intercept them by cultivating our minds and skills. Too often we expect to receive and execute an idea in a field we have no understanding of. If today, God delivered to you, in your sleep, the complete plans for cheaply producing a car that runs fully on water, could you do it? Not likely, unless you already possessed a significant understanding of automobiles and energy systems. In other words, it is almost impossible to adapt something you have not adopted. Women often have great ideas about how a household appliance could work better. Their ideas come from the repeated use of those machines and the frustrations they experienced. If they do not go out and implement those ideas, they will die with them.

Man's Part

> 'The silver is mine and the gold is mine,' declares the Lord Almighty. **Haggai 2:8 (NIV)**

> For every animal of the forest is mine, and the cattle on a thousand hills. **Psalm 50:10 (NIV)**

All wealth belongs to God. That includes the wealth in the hands of people and nations that do not believe in God. God created our minds, our hands, and the land that we work on. Without Him, it would be impossible for us to exist or be wealthy; God makes all things possible. When God gives you and me money, he intends that the money be used in the service of His purpose. And to ensure that everything He gives to us will be used for his glory He reserves a bit of all that He gives to us for Himself. After He has blessed us, God commands us to take a part of what He gave us and bring it back to Him. Our willingness and diligence in giving back this little portion is proof to God that we will use the rest of our God-given wealth for what is right. It is easy to claim that your money belongs to God but unless you are faithful in giving God what belongs to Him, that claim is not true.

There are three levels in the giving of our material possessions as an act of worship. They are:

- Tithing
- Offerings
- Vows

Understanding the role and importance of these three elements is important for obtaining and securing material prosperity. No part of this world and hence our lives is demilitarized; every part is either a territory for God or Satan. By failing to obey the word of God in our finances, we declare our money to not be under His jurisdiction. In not committing sexual immorality, we demonstrate God's authority over our bodies. By not thinking the wrong thoughts, we demonstrate God's authority over our minds. Through being careful in our friendships, we show God's authority over our relationships. By tithing our income, we demonstrate God's authority over our finances. In the next chapter, we will discuss the spiritual significance of tithes, offerings, vows, various financial seeds and the power of charitable deeds.

CHAPTER EIGHT: DIVINE BLUEPRINT FOR WEALTH; YOUR PART

There is no more controversial subject in church than the issue of money. Due to many people's religious backgrounds they have been conditioned to expect that anything spiritual or holy must be dissociated from money. They view a religious teacher or church leader who talks about money and engages in money-making activities as worldly. A really spiritual person should isolate themselves from mundane things that are likely to impede their ability to communicate with God. They claim that it is impossible to be out in the world doing everyday things and still be holy. People put spirituality into a category and everyday living into another, without both ever mixing. So when a church talks about money, it is viewed as unspiritual.– People attitudes affect how they give to God; since money is filthy and unspiritual, it is unwise to have too much of it in the church, lest it corrupts the truth.

This idea is the invention of Satan, through the greed of ungodly politicians who want to stifle the church and rob it of influence. Politicians would rather the money people gave to God came to them. They want to obstruct the church's ability to influence society by participating in business and politics. They realize the church would be a formidable adversary if it ever used its population and influence. The best way to keep the church under control is to starve it of money by convincing people that God and money are irreconcilable. By promoting the idea that the church has no business getting involved in the legislative process. In recent years however, the church has started to throw off these limitations as preachers, as well as church people begin to view politics and enterprise as legitimate instruments for changing the world.

> Be shepherds of God's flock that is under your care, watching over them—not because you must, but because you are willing, as God wants you to be; not pursuing dishonest gain, but eager to serve; **1 Peter 5:2 (NIV)**

> Their destiny is destruction, their god is their stomach, and their glory is in their shame. Their mind is set on earthly things. **Philippians 3:19 (NIV)**

Satan has not watched these developments idly; he has responded by perverting God's truths about the use of money in the lives of believers. The distortion of God's truth has led many Pastors to live more like celebrities in the secular world than as ministers of God's word. Their messages and lifestyles promote materialism and money has become the main subject of their teaching and the only way to obtain a blessing from God. Instead of leading people to righteousness, obedience, compassion and faith as foundations of Godly living, their preaching is all about what people should give and what they can get. This new reality is the reason a lot of church folks are suspicious of any discussions about money in the church. Yet, money does have a valid role in God's plans for the church and it is our responsibility to discover what this is. The truth is this, as we have abandoned the paths of materialism, we also give up the position of viewing money as separate from spirituality. Instead we must now advance to a new position that is truly founded on the Word of God.

The Tithe

> Honor the Lord with your wealth, with the firstfruits of all your crops; then your barns will be filled to overflowing, and your vats

will brim over with new wine. **Proverbs 3:9-10 (NIV)**

Bring the whole tithe into the storehouse, that there may be food in my house. Test me in this," says the Lord Almighty, "and see if I will not throw open the floodgates of heaven and pour out so much blessing that there will not be room enough to store it. I will prevent pests from devouring your crops, and the vines in your fields will not drop their fruit before it is ripe," says the Lord Almighty. **Malachi 3:10-11 (NIV)**

What is the tithe and why should you pay it? There is no wealth without obligations and responsibility because there is no prosperity that is not linked to a source. The origin of that wealth will always demand a part of it as its due and a token to acknowledge its contribution to the process. This is true when investors give money to a company; they expect something back. Gifts create an obligation; a cycle that is only complete when the receiver meets that obligation. Parents automatically gain a right to exercise a measure of authority over their children because the children came into life through the parents and depend on them for guidance, food, shelter, clothing and other things. In return for what they provide, parents demand loyalty and obedience. If the child does not return these to the parents, the relationship is fractured. The same relates to God; whatever He gives to us creates a debt of worship and service. If we do not return these to Him we have broken the cycle and ruptured the relationship.

Be sure to set aside a tenth of all that your fields produce each year. **Deuteronomy 14:22 (NIV)**

As discussed earlier, God gives us 'power to get wealth' and as we begin to experience the benefits of that blessing, He mandates us to return a portion of it to him. That part we give back to God is a token to acknowledge that we recognize Him as the source and sustainer of our wealth. It demonstrates that we consider our wisdom, enterprise, health and happiness as a stream that is linked to the river of His Grace. We are saying we know that if we were ever cut off from that source, everything we are would wither and die. The Tithe is not something that we give to God. It is God's property. He has stipulated that ten percent of our income is His expected returns from the investment He made in our lives. The tithe is an obligation. It is something that God fixed in His authority and accepting this is accepting His Lordship.

> But keep away from the devoted things, so that you will not bring about your own destruction by taking any of them. Otherwise you will make the camp of Israel liable to destruction and bring trouble on it. **Joshua 6:18 (NIV)**

Tithing is proof of our obedience and submission to God. Other than through the tithe, there is no way to show that the authority of God extends over our finances. When we remove the tithe from our income, we ensure that what is left is blessed. It is not only blessed but becomes more than sufficient for our needs. When we fail to obey God in tithing, we put our wealth in a pocket with holes because things show up that steal our money. Our lives will be attended with unexpected misfortunes that drain away our resources. This happens because we have allowed our money to become cursed. But God says if we give Him His part, He will protect us from things that could devour our wealth. Finally, paying the tithe promotes personal discipline and fiscal responsibility. If you can diligently take out the ten percent, then you can also delay gratification and save your money; vital qualities for wealth-building.

Offerings

> The kings of the earth are bringing their gifts to your Temple in Jerusalem. **Psalm 68:29 (TLB)**

> Fulfill all your vows that you have made to Jehovah your God. Let everyone bring him presents. He should be reverenced and feared. **Psalm 76:11 (TLB)**

While tithing tests our obedience, offerings reveal our gratitude. Offerings demonstrate how much we freely ascribe our blessings to God. There is no compulsion with the offering, so it is an accurate revelation of how we really feel in our hearts. When we have a celebration, we use the value of the gifts people give us as an assessment of their love and happiness for us. An average gift from a rich person rates lower than a cheap gift from a poor person who saved their money to buy us that gift. The gifts people give us reveal the worth they place on their relationship with us. Thus offerings offer a window into the value we place on what we are getting from God. It says whether we feel that we have received much or little. The tithe cannot measure this because it is a fixed rate and is commanded. Offerings, on the other hand, depend on free will.

> Each of you must bring a gift in proportion to the way the Lord your God has blessed you. **Deuteronomy 16:17 (NIV)**

> Celebrate the Festival of Unleavened Bread; for seven days eat bread made without yeast, as I commanded you. Do this at the appointed time in the month of Aviv, for in

> that month you came out of Egypt. No one is to appear before me empty-handed. **Exodus 23:15 (NIV)**

Offerings are a way to honor the presence of our King. It is customary when visiting a dignitary, such as a Monarch, an elected politician, a country's ambassador or a respected leader, to bear gifts. It is the protocol of the court and without a gift you would never be admitted to see the monarch. Before the visitor is brought before the Monarch, their gifts would be presented. The worth of their gifts determines the predisposition of the King or Queen toward them. These gifts are not given to meet the needs of the ruler; they demonstrate honor. In our modern age, we like to think that we have gone past these rituals but it is not true. A person who bears gifts inspires in us a desire to please. We are motivated to give them more than they need because their gifts have elevated them in our sight. We are not giving to feed their hunger but to make them happy. We give more to people who give us gifts.

Vows

> I will come to your temple with burnt offerings and fulfill my vows to you—vows my lips promised and my mouth spoke when I was in trouble. **Psalm 66:13-14 (NIV)**

> Then Israel made this vow to the Lord: "If you will deliver these people into our hands, we will totally destroy their cities." **Numbers 21:2 (NIV)**

On occasion, we encounter stories in the Bible where someone makes a vow to do something for God if He does a particular thing for that person. Vows are a way to trigger a divine response to an intractable problem. They are often actions of last resort; something that the person does after exhausting all other legitimate options. The person involved has obeyed the word of God regarding the situation to no avail. Vows become necessary when an element of the miraculous is required to change a situation. A vow is not a bribe; it is an overextension of oneself in order to convince God to also overextend Himself on behalf of the person. Through a vow we can demonstrate to God that we are willing to go past the ordinary level of commitment expected from us in exchange for a higher level of intervention than He usually gives.

> And she made a vow, saying, "Lord Almighty, if you will only look on your servant's misery and remember me, and not forget your servant but give her a son, then I will give him to the Lord for all the days of his life, and no razor will ever be used on his head." **1 Samuel 1:11 (NIV)**

Vows are used when seeking extraordinary blessings. In all facets of life, to receive something special, a person must do something special. There is a minimum requirement that God places on us in order to bless us. If we keep those requirements, God is obligated to respond. But when we want more than He promised, we must give more than He asks. Similarly, vows can be used to break strong afflictions. We can secure a higher level of supernatural intervention in our situation by making a heartfelt commitment to do something beyond the ordinary for God. In the story of Hannah, the curse of barrenness was broken because she promised to give the son back to God's service. At that time, God was looking for someone to replace the aging priest, Eli, who had betrayed Him along with his sons. Through her vow, Hannah secured God by her side as an ally because God now had something to gain by her getting pregnant.

Where To Give Tithes and Offerings

> Bring the whole tithe ... that there may be <u>food in my house</u>. **Malachi 3:10 (NIV)**

Should tithes and offerings always be given to a church? Is it alright to give my tithes to the poor? These are questions church folks sometimes ask. As stated, the tithe belongs to God and He alone can designate who receives the tithe on His behalf. In the natural sense, only a government can determine the collecting authority for taxes and other payments. The tithe, God's money, is reserved by God for the use of people who work for Him, to enable them to continue doing His work. God uses the tithe to pay His earthly staff and maintain the services necessary for their continued ministry. By tithing in the place where you worship, you ensure that the society continues to have the benefit of its work. In reality, the tithe goes back to the persons who gave it because it ensures that they continue to have the benefits of ministry.

> "I give to the Levites all the tithes in Israel as their inheritance in return for the work they do while serving at the tent of meeting. **Numbers 18:21 (NIV)**

> I also learned that the portions assigned to the Levites had not been given to them, and that all the Levites and musicians responsible for the service had gone back to their own fields. **Nehemiah 13:10 (NIV)**

Secondly, the church is the minister of the '*power to get*'; the grace of God flows to you through their ministry. If someone was the instrument by which you become blessed, it is only right that you share that blessing with the person. To do otherwise would break the cycle. Just as the river feeds the sea, the sea feeds the rain, and the rain feeds underground springs that in turn feed the river, so our giving feeds the system that brings rain into our lives. A disruption of any part of the system would result in the failure of the whole. Giving to the poor has its own benefits. When we give to the poor, we give a blessing, rather than respond to a blessing received. Tithes and offerings complete a process that is already in motion. Based on the significance of offerings, it makes no sense to give them in any other setting than when we gather to our King. If you have problems with giving your tithes and offerings where you worship, maybe you should find another place where you will be comfortable with giving your money. However, if you feel leaving is not an option, then you should deal with the roots of your reluctance. If the church is not managing the funds well, then demand for greater accountability from the leadership.

The Principle of Exchange

Everything God created carries seed and has a need. The seed is the blessing that it gives to the world; the need is what it takes from the world. There is nothing God made which is self-sufficient; everything needs some other thing to survive. In order to get what the other has, it must offer something of its own. Without this exchange, there would be no relationships and the whole world would stop functioning. Every time someone gives something, they create a vacuum in their treasures. That vacuum is only filled by the person who received what they gave, reciprocating with something different but commensurate. Where the second person is unwilling to give something, the first will be reluctant to give anything also. If the second person goes ahead to take what the first has without payment, it is called stealing.

> Our desire is not that others might be relieved while you are hard pressed, but that

> there might be equality. At the present time your plenty will supply what they need, so that in turn their plenty will supply what you need. The goal is equality, as it is written: "The one who gathered much did not have too much, and the one who gathered little did not have too little." **2 Corinthians 8:13-15 (NIV)**

This principle is true for both physical and spiritual exchanges. Everyone is designed to be a champion of their own gifts and abilities. No one can become a true champion without the other person becoming a champion too. The champion businessman needs the champion tailor, who needs the champion baker, and so on. The system works if each person is able to dedicate themselves to becoming good at what they do, safe in the knowledge that the things they do not do will be done by others. They can now exchange what they have made for what others have made and live as though they were champions in every area of life. This is easy to understand when dealing with tangible goods or services. It is much harder to understand in relation to spiritual things.

> If we have sown spiritual seed among you, is it too much if we reap a material harvest from you? **1 Corinthians 9:11 (NIV)**

People sometimes wonder what those with spiritual gifts contribute. What does one get for giving their concrete goods in exchange for unseen spiritual gifts? The value of the spiritual is not realized until it is taken away. People did not see the effect of prayer in schools until it was removed. By God's systems, we always exchange what we have for something we desire. To receive the full benefits of spiritual ministry, we give something too. If we do not do this, the exchange is invalid and does not happen. This is one reason two persons can experience the same ministry with vastly different results. Unlike physical goods, spiritual virtue cannot be stolen. It is transferred to the proportion to which we value the vessel. In the Bible people going to consult with a prophet always carried a gift. To get more, you have to do more.

> From everyone who has been given much, much will be demanded; and from the one who has been entrusted with much, much more will be asked. **Luke 12:48 (NIV)**

Acts of Charity

> But when you give a banquet, invite the poor, the crippled, the lame, the blind, and you will be blessed. Although they cannot repay you, you will be repaid ..." **Luke 14:13-14 (NIV)**

Tithing tests obedience and offerings test gratitude but charity tests generosity. When we realize that grace plays a much bigger role in our accomplishments than efforts, we learn the importance of helping others. It is easy to attribute our achievements to our intelligence. Serendipity plays a bigger role than we can understand. What are the odds that you could have found the great relationship you now have, without a chance meeting? How many times have you been one inch from calamity and saved by an unseen hand? The reality is most of the good things that happen in our lives are stumbled into. They, more often than not, pop up on the road; surprising, interrupting and engaging our attention. When we realize the hand of providence silently working behind the scenes of our lives, we become less judgmental and more accommodating of the less privileged.

> "Then the King will say to those on his right, 'Come, you who are blessed by my

Father; take your inheritance, the kingdom prepared for you since the creation of the world. For I was hungry and you gave me something to eat, I was thirsty and you gave me something to drink, I was a stranger and you invited me in, I needed clothes and you clothed me, I was sick and you looked after me, I was in prison and you came to visit me.' "Then the righteous will answer him, 'Lord, when did we see you hungry and feed you, or thirsty and give you something to drink? When did we see you a stranger and invite you in, or needing clothes and clothe you? When did we see you sick or in prison and go to visit you?' "The King will reply, 'Truly I tell you, whatever you did for one of the least of these brothers and sisters of mine, you did for me.' **Matthew 25:34-40 (NIV)**

Poor people are a test of our character. We do not have to be nice or generous to them since we are not expecting anything from them. The humanity of a society is shown by how it treats those who have little to contribute. A society that treats the poor and weak badly slowly kills itself through the destruction of empathy. That society will descend into a place where people are measured by things and the desperation of people to avoid poverty will lead to overflowing violence. When we deny the poor of their humanity, we destroy the tranquility of our society. Helping the poor is helping yourself because it preserves you as a human being. It keeps you humble and strengthens your compassion. It allows you to stay in a place where you can feel the pain of others. If you deny the cry of a stranger in the street, it becomes easier to ignore the pain of your loved ones at home. We cannot be selectively compassionate.

> Whoever is kind to the poor lends to the Lord, and he will reward them for what they have done. **Proverbs 19:17 (NIV)**

The person who gives to the poor does more for themselves than they do for the person they help. They build a hedge around their own success by reducing the number of thieves trying to take away their success. The bible says that poor people are the responsibility of God; He looks out for the orphan, the widow and the stranger. When we help such people, we are doing God's work for Him. Because we have taken from our resources and given to those who are in need. He now diverts His own resources back to us. This is how that works; the orphan, widow and immigrant are at a disadvantage because they lack the means to draw wealth into their lives. Since God needs a physical medium that He can pour the spiritual blessing into, such as land, job, business, connections or skills. But these people lack those things and so God is unable to bless them directly. However, when we give to them, we have assumed God's responsibilities and in repayment God now diverts the spiritual blessings he should have given to these people into our hands through our work, business, relationships and God-given ideas. That way our giving creates balance; we extend generosity to the poor and God extends blessings to us; creating peace in our lands.

CHAPTER NINE: STEWARDSHIP

The Lord your God will certainly make a lasting dynasty for my lord, because you fight the Lord's battles, and no wrongdoing will be found in you as long as you live. **1 Samuel 25:28 (NIV)**

David asked the men standing near him, "What will be done for the man who kills this Philistine and removes this disgrace from Israel? Who is this uncircumcised Philistine that he should defy the armies of the living God?" **1 Samuel 17:26 (NIV)**

The biggest key to wealth is to offer oneself as a dedicated vessel to the advancement of God's agenda. When you do this, your battle becomes God's and His resources become yours. This was the biggest secret of King David; he was dedicated to fighting God's battles. His disposition toward anybody was determined by that person's attitude to God. The reason he challenged Goliath was that he felt personally insulted by the words the giant spoke against God. While others could ignore the insolence of the Philistine, David was willing to risk life and limb to vindicate God. As a result of his willingness to go the extra mile for God, he was entrusted with the Kingdom and God gave him custody over vast resources and a great number of nations. This was a quality David had previously demonstrated as a shepherd guarding the sheep; he could not turn a blind eye to the injustice of a lion killing a lamb.

> "I am the good shepherd. The good shepherd lays down his life for the sheep. **John 10:11 (NIV)**

> For zeal for your house consumes me, and the insults of those who insult you fall on me. **Psalm 69:9 (NIV)**

God is looking for men and women to whom He will commit the treasures of knowledge, money and relationships needed to do His work. The question is; will we be faithful or will we use the resources of God to satisfy our personal ambitions, like King Saul? David recognized that He was given power for the benefit of people and he set out to use that power to create justice and equity. Saul used the power to massage his ego and build a personal dynasty. The difference between King Saul and King David is the reason the Messiah is likened to David; Jesus is the ultimate steward. He gives up His life for the Sheep. He was consumed by the zeal for God's house. The extent that we are willing to go for God's glory is the extent to which he will elevate and empower us.

> Who then is the faithful and wise servant, whom the master has put in charge of the servants in his household to give them their food at the proper time? **Matthew 24:45 (NIV)**

> Now it is required that those who have been given a trust must prove faithful. **1 Corinthians 4:2 (NIV)**

The key word in the first Bible quote above is 'put in charge.' This means that God will give what is His into the control of a person because He can trust him. He can trust him to be faithful in managing it because he has character. He can trust him not to lose God's resources because he has competence. This person becomes a treasurer of heaven and a conduit by which blessings are distributed all around the world. That was the kind of relationship that Abraham enjoyed with God; he was blessed to be a blessing to the nations. Abraham earned that position by gaining trust through consistent obedience. The number one reason why there are not many believers who own great enterprises and control vast amounts of wealth is that we have not demonstrated to God that we would know what to do with His resources if trusted with them. It is not enough to hold wealth in trust, it is also important to know how to use it effectively. Ask yourself this; if God put you in charge of twenty million dollars of His money, where would you invest it?

> To one he gave five bags of gold, to another two bags, and to another one bag, each according to his ability. Then he went on his journey. **Matthew 25:15 (NIV)**

Cultivating The Character of A Steward

While you may not be at the level where God can commit large wealth into your hands, you do have something over which you are a steward. Recognize that everything you have been given is actually committed into your hand for safekeeping. The bible says that if we are faithful in small things, we will be promoted to handle big things. The amount of resources and blessing you currently manage reflect the level of trust you have demonstrated in managing things. Your relationships; spouse, children, friends, relatives and connections, are all responsibilities. Your material possessions; home, money, car and other assets, are responsibilities. Your own self; health, intellect and abilities, are responsibilities. If you manage a few people well, you prove that you can manage a community. If you manage your money well, you demonstrate that you can manage a business. If you manage yourself well, you show evidence that you can lead others.

The conflict with lions and bears prepared David for the encounter with Goliath. Defeating Goliath prepared him to become a celebrated general. Becoming adept at war, enabled him to manage the responsibilities of Kingship. Every step and place in your life builds on the last one and prepares you for the next one. If you fail to fully master the challenges of your current level of life, you disqualify yourself for the higher level. Until you excel at the current test, you will not get a promotion to the next. Sometimes people force themselves into the next level of life by faking, buying or stealing it. The strategy never works because the qualities needed for living and performing at that level cannot be bought, stolen or faked. They are only acquired through the process of failing, trying and finally learning. Such people ultimately crash and burn.

> Whoever can be trusted with very little can also be trusted with much, and whoever is dishonest with very little will also be dishonest with much. **Luke 16:10 (NIV)**

How do you prepare yourself to become a great steward? By cultivating contentment; which is the ability to stay at peace and give your best in whatever position you are in life. When you view every situation as a learning experience, an opportunity to serve and a stepping board to your next level, you will give your best rather than fret. You should endeavor to cultivate the attitude of seeing yourself as serving God rather than men. This means that God is the one who holds the stages of your life and determines where you will be at any point. Therefore where you are now was not the decision of other people but a place God assigned you to for a purpose. Although you cannot see that purpose, make it your goal to do your best in that situation. By doing this you will soon outgrow that place and be automatically called to a higher position.

> So whether you eat or drink or whatever you do, do it all for the glory of God. **1 Corinthians 10:31 (NIV)**

> But when you are invited, take the lowest place, so that when your host comes, he will say to you, 'Friend, move up to a better place.' Then you will be honored in the presence of all the other guests. **Luke 14:10 (NIV)**

The Qualities of a Steward

Trustworthiness

The steward must be dependable. To be dependable means to have a steady character - that person is predictable in a positive way. It means that the master can make his plans with you as a central part of it without any fear of you disappointing him. A dependable character comes from consistent habits, which are the results of a person having gained mastery over their appetites and emotions.

> Putting confidence in an unreliable man is like chewing with a sore tooth, or trying to run on a broken foot. **Proverbs 25:19 (TLB)**

Loyalty

The steward will never act in contradiction to the master's vision, plans or instructions. Stewards are trusted allies who always work for the benefit of the boss. Stewards protect the interest of the one they work for, even when their superior commits an error.

> Most people will tell you what loyal friends they are, but are they telling the truth? **Proverbs 20:6 (TLB)**

Accountability

Stewards must have a record of the resources and people at their disposal. Stewards should be able to tell to what uses the resources in their care were put. The steward is not wasteful but squeezes the maximum benefit out of every cent.

> Jesus told his disciples: "There was a rich man whose manager was accused of wasting his possessions. So he called him in and asked him, 'What is this I hear about you? Give an account of your management, because you cannot be manager any longer.'
> **Luke 16:1-2 (NIV)**

Skillful

A steward must possess the competence to manage people and resources. Stewards have to be good at making decisions. Stewards are similar to a manager of funds; it is their responsibility to protect the master's assets and secure him the most profits. Stewards must be prudent and shrewd.

> All who are skilled among you are to come and make everything the Lord has commanded: **Exodus 35:10 (NIV)**

Moderation

The steward cannot use the assets in his keeping for the satisfaction of his personal desires. A portion of the resources committed to a steward goes to meeting his/her needs. The steward must be able to control his/her appetite, spending only the money assigned to personal needs for that purpose. The master's wealth is not for gratification and self-promotion.

> Everyone who competes in the games goes into strict training. They do it to get a crown that will not last, but we do it to get a crown that will last forever. **1 Corinthians 9:25 (NIV)**

Benefits of Good Financial Stewardship

There is power in the ability to keep back a bit of whatever one earns. There is a phenomenon easily observable in life; people who live from check to check, become poorer and poorer; but those who make a habit of not spending all that they get, become richer. This is not always because the second group accumulates more money through their savings. Rather, what happens is that they receive more opportunities to save even more. They also begin to find investments to which they can put their savings and earn even more. As a result, without really increasing their income, they are able to grow their assets. Additionally, cultivating the habit of keeping back money builds a person's ability to control their appetite and delay gratification. They are able to exercise greater control over themselves and over their lives. Below are some benefits of good stewardship of our money.

<u>A Hedge Against Trouble</u>: A store of wealth provides a hedge against future uncertainties. If a person loses their source of income, the depth of their assets determine how many days into the future they can live without becoming destitute. If you cannot survive up to three months without a job, you are living a high-risk life. Money may not buy happiness but money can prevent some unhappiness.

> A person's riches may ransom their life, but the poor cannot respond to threatening rebukes. **Proverbs 13:8 (NIV)**

A War Chest: Money in store serves as a war chest to combat different categories of trouble. Money will ward off hunger and can buy you allies and protection. Money can even secure health. A person with no treasure is prey to all circumstances that come their way.

> Wisdom is a shelter as money is a shelter, but the advantage of knowledge is this: Wisdom preserves those who have it. **Ecclesiastes 7:12 (NIV)**

Peace Versus Anxiety: When a person has properly managed the resources that have passed through their hands and not spent it all, they purchase peace for themselves. They do not have anxiety about what will happen if their circumstances suddenly change.

> When it snows, she has no fear for her household; for all of them are clothed in scarlet. **Proverbs 31:21 (NIV)**

> Surely the righteous will never be shaken; they will be remembered forever. They will have no fear of bad news; their hearts are steadfast, trusting in the Lord. **Psalm 112:6-7 (NIV)**

Ability To Seize Opportunities: Money or wealth in store allows one to take opportunities. How many times have you encountered a chance of a lifetime and could not take it because you had no money? The best opportunities in life come unexpectedly.

> "Then, just as the Lord had said, my cousin Hanamel came to me in the courtyard of the guard and said, 'Buy my field at Anathoth in the territory of Benjamin. Since it is your right to redeem it and possess it, buy it for

yourself.' "I knew that this was the word of the Lord; **Jeremiah 32:8 (NIV)**

Business Capital: Many of the global brands that we see today began with money saved by the owners of the business, as well as some borrowed from the savings of friends and families. The Chinese economic miracle was financed by citizen's savings.

> The wise store up choice food and olive oil, but fools gulp theirs down. **Proverbs 21:20 (NIV)**

Endow Good Causes: There is never a want of noble causes needing contributions from decent citizens. The problem is that there is a shortage of good people who have the money to do so. Well-managed resources enable you to make a difference where it matters most.

> Besides, in my devotion to the temple of my God I now give my personal treasures of gold and silver for the temple of my God, over and above everything I have provided for this holy temple: **1 Chronicles 29:3 (NIV)**

An Inheritance for Children: By prudently managing the resources you have today, you provide a better starting point for your children in life. Assess to assets is always an advantage and will give any young person a head start in life.

> A good person leaves an inheritance for their children's children, but a sinner's wealth is stored up for the righteous. **Proverbs 13:22 (NIV)**

<u>Build Generational Wealth</u>: Prudence in the handling your investments can create compounding wealth that crosses generational lines. By using what you have properly; you can kick-start the building of a financial dynasty.

> Their children will be mighty in the land;
> the generation of the upright will be blessed.
> **Psalm 112:2 (NIV)**

The Wise person prepares for winter when it is summer. As the saying goes 'make hay while the sun shines.' Many of the old people who become destitute did not get that way because they lacked opportunities in their younger years. Typically it is due to misused chances.

> I have seen a grievous evil under the sun: wealth hoarded to the harm of its owners, or wealth lost through some misfortune, so that when they have children there is nothing left for them to inherit. **Ecclesiastes 5:13-14 (NIV)**

CHAPTER TEN: ROADBLOCKS TO YOUR PAYDAY

Your fight for financial prosperity is not your struggle alone; it is an extension of the conflict between good and evil. Satan wants all of mankind, especially the children of God, to languish in the prison of poverty. He has the most interest in keeping Spirit-filled and Bible-living believers from realizing their potential. To keep you impotent, Satan deploys a range of weapons against you. These could be your own history, experiences and weaknesses. Or it could be relationships and the forces of witchcraft. Whatever it is, you owe it to yourself, your loved ones, society and God to fight till you gain the whole blessing of God reserved for you. The list below serves as a guideline to help you to look deeper into your life and identify areas where you need to make improvements. The list is divided into different categories of obstacles.

Spiritual Roadblocks

Your effort for wealth is not a physical battle. Although we operate in the physical dimension and use natural tools, we do not draw power from these sources. It might appear as if spirituality has no direct connection to success. This is not true because your whole life takes origin from your spirit. The stronger your spirit is, the more power you will have at your disposal to follow the right course. The people you encounter as you pursue wealth are not alone; they often have the backing of demonic spirits. To be effective, you must fight against:

<u>Living Without God's Word</u>: The word of God gives your life and desires meaning. Without it, you will lose sight of what is right and true. Studying and meditating on God's word keeps your life centered, your efforts focused and your heart humble.

> My son, pay attention to what I say; turn your ear to my words. Do not let them out of your sight, keep them within your heart; for they are life to those who find them and health to one's whole body. **Proverbs 4:20-22 (NIV)**

> Your word is a lamp for my feet, a light on my path. **Psalm 119:105 (NIV)**

<u>Failure to Pray Regularly</u>: There will be many times when you will face tough situations and decisions. Or find yourself grappling with strong temptation. Making a habit of prayer will help you to find insight and strength to overcome the worst difficulties.

> Watch and pray so that you will not fall into temptation. The spirit is willing, but the flesh is weak. **Matthew 26:41 (NIV)**

> The prayer of a righteous person is powerful and effective. **James 5:16b (NIV)**

<u>Ignoring The Holy Spirit</u>: No one owns complete knowledge of any situation, there are gaps in our best plans. By listening to the promptings of the Holy Spirit, you protect yourself from making catastrophic decisions that may seem right at the time.

> Teach me to do your will, for you are my God; may your good Spirit lead me on level ground. **Psalm 143:10 (NIV)**

> For those who are led by the Spirit of God are the children of God. **Romans 8:14 (NIV)**

Lacking Integrity: When we have integrity, our life will have congruence. There will be an agreement between what we think, say and do. A person who lacks integrity is short-sighted and their success will be short-lived.

> The integrity of the upright guides them, but the unfaithful are destroyed by their duplicity. **Proverbs 11:3 (NIV)**

> keeping a clear conscience, so that those who speak maliciously against your good behavior in Christ may be ashamed of their slander. **1 Peter 3:16 (NIV)**

Dominated by Competitiveness: If your motive for wanting prosperity is to outshine others or spite them, you are likely to fail. That kind of thinking leads people to do anything for money because they have to have it now. Such people cannot endure the process.

> And I saw that all toil and all achievement spring from one person's envy of another. This too is meaningless, a chasing after the wind. **Ecclesiastes 4:4 (NIV)**

> We do not dare to classify or compare ourselves with some who commend themselves. When they measure themselves by themselves and compare themselves with themselves, they are not wise. **2 Corinthians 10:12 (NIV)**

Fear and Unbelief: Your faith is the channel through which God's promises reach you. Satan attacks your faith to stop you from acting on God's word. A fearful mind is already defeated before the fight begins. The world floods your mind daily with things that create fear, self-doubt and feelings of helplessness. But when you constantly imbibe the word of God and fellowship with the Holy Spirit, you will be filled with power rather than fear.

> Fear of man will prove to be a snare, but whoever trusts in the Lord is kept safe. **Proverbs 29:25 (NIV)**
>
> And he did not do many miracles there because of their lack of faith. **Matthew 13:58 (NIV)**
>
> Let us hold unswervingly to the hope we profess, for he who promised is faithful. **Hebrews 10:23 (NIV)**

<u>Greed and Selfishness</u>: Wealth is a result of what you contribute to the life of others. If you dedicate yourself to making others happier, healthier and better, you have also earned the right to be healthy, happy and better. Too often, people are looking for what they can take and are blinded to the wealth opportunities that exist around them; because opportunities come as an invitation to do something for another person. If you are too focused on yourself, you cannot make something of value to others and will therefore have nothing to exchange for money.

> Whoever loves money never has enough; whoever loves wealth is never satisfied with their income. This too is meaningless. **Ecclesiastes 5:10 (NIV)**
>
> For where you have envy and selfish ambition, there you find disorder and every evil practice. **James 3:16 (NIV)**
>
> Those who trust in their riches will fall, but the righteous will thrive like a green leaf. **Proverbs 11:28 (NIV)**

Ancestral curses: Forces that you have no knowledge of can serve as a weight to pull you back from success. These are spirits which gain access to your life through past relationships and experiences. To become all that God wants you to be you must disconnect from such powers. I discuss how to do this in great detail in my book *'**Gracefully Broken**: Freedom from pain and generational curses through humility, inner healing and deliverance.'*

Relationship Roadblocks

Everyone that you habitually relate to is a door - they serve as points through which spirits gain access to you. Whatever spiritual influences those people yield themselves to; they will attempt to transmit to you in turn. Judge your relationships by the emotions and actions that they reinforce in you. Watch out for the following relationship roadblocks.

Negative People: This includes naysayers who try to keep you from pursuing your goals. Such people are usually not doing much with their lives. Having people around them who are failing makes them feel better about themselves. Other kinds of negative relationships are those that reinforce lifestyles and habits that go against the fulfillment of your vision. They encourage your weaknesses.

> Stay away from a fool, for you will not find knowledge on their lips. **Proverbs 14:7 (NIV)**

> Walk with the wise and become wise, for a companion of fools suffers harm. **Proverbs 13:20 (NIV)**

Wrong Environments: Negative relationships do not always involve people who are close to you. Merely by living in an environment contradictory to winning, success becomes harder. This is because environments create systems that support the values uppermost in the minds of those who live in them. Environments exert a gravitational pull on those inside them.

> Better is one day in your courts than a thousand elsewhere; I would rather be a doorkeeper in the house of my God than dwell in the tents of the wicked. **Psalm 84:10 (NIV)**

> Do not be misled: Bad company corrupts good character. **1 Corinthians 15:33 (NIV)**

> As iron sharpens iron, so one person sharpens another. **Proverbs 27:17 (NIV)**

Divided Forces: When you attempt to pursue a dream with someone who does not share the same values as you or is not as motivated by the goal, you sabotage your own success. Never let emotional attachments or fear of going alone drive you into partnerships with people who do not care about the things you care about.

> Do two walk together unless they have agreed to do so? **Amos 3:3 (NIV)**

> Do not be yoked together with unbelievers. For what do righteousness and wickedness have in common? Or what fellowship can light have with darkness? **2 Corinthians 6:14 (NIV)**

Speaking Only One Language: People can create a ceiling for their own success by being unable to relate outside their circle. If you cannot accommodate others people's difference, your success will be average. Being able to interact with dissimilar people does not alter who you are. Relate with people on the basis of their similarities with you and not their differences.

Now Hiram king of Tyre sent envoys to David, along with cedar logs and carpenters and stonemasons, and they built a palace for David. **2 Samuel 5:11 (NIV)**

When Hiram king of Tyre heard that Solomon had been anointed king to succeed his father David, he sent his envoys to Solomon, because he had always been on friendly terms with David. **1 Kings 5:1 (NIV)**

<u>Underestimating People</u>; Even if a person does not have money, they may know something you do not or may be connected to someone you need. There is no human being who is completely without worth. The failure to cultivate a habit of treating everyone with respect will shut your doors. By taking an interest in other people, you will constantly be expanding your network, as well as your opportunities.

Show proper respect to everyone…**1 Peter 2:17a (NIV)**

Suppose a man comes into your meeting wearing a gold ring and fine clothes, and a poor man in filthy old clothes also comes in. If you show special attention to the man wearing fine clothes and say, "Here's a good seat for you," but say to the poor man, "You stand there" or "Sit on the floor by my feet," have you not discriminated among yourselves and become judges with evil thoughts? **James 2:2-4 (NIV)**

Do not forget to show hospitality to strangers, for by so doing some people have shown hospitality to angels without knowing it. **Hebrews 13:2 (NIV)**

Developmental Roadblocks

You are the most important factor in your own success. Everything that God brings into your hands must pass through your spirit and mind. The extent to which you develop yourself is the extent to which you will be able to receive and keep the blessing of God. The greater your capacity, the more responsibility you will be given.

> If the ax is dull and its edge unsharpened, more strength is needed, but skill will bring success. **Ecclesiastes 10:10 (NIV)**

<u>Lacking Positive Life Focus</u>: Your life moves in the direction of your highest goals. Your mind and energies bend toward the things you elevate. A life goal is a compass, map and power source. Focus forces you to find direction; the things that engage your heart will make you gravitate towards people, places and experiences that help you reach the goal. A goal weeds out wrong behaviors and people from your life.

> Let your eyes look straight ahead; fix your gaze directly before you. Give careful thought to the paths for your feet and be steadfast in all your ways. Do not turn to the right or the left; keep your foot from evil. **Proverbs 4:25-27 (NIV)**

<u>Low or No Skills</u>: Skills allow you to provide value. Definitions of skill: *An ability that has been acquired by training* or *Ability to produce solutions in some problem domain*. The two important components of skill are training and problem-solving. Training is not going to school but repeatedly applying oneself to something; it is the process of getting better by doing. The second aspect of skill is problem-solving. The level of solutions your skills provide determines how much people will pay for them.

> To one he gave five bags of gold, to another two bags, and to another one bag, each according to his ability. Then he went on his journey. **Matthew 25:15 (NIV)**

> "He replied, 'I tell you that to everyone who has, more will be given, but as for the one who has nothing, even what they have will be taken away. **Luke 19:26 (NIV)**

Underdeveloped Abilities: When you connect skill to talent, you amplify impact and multiply your opportunities for wealth. Identifying what you are good at and monetizing it makes wealth easier to come by. Before talent can create money, it must be transformed into skill. Unless you work hard at your natural abilities, they will be unproductive. As a matter of fact, a hardworking person with no talent will outperform a talented person who doesn't work hard.

> For this reason I remind you to fan into flame the gift of God, which is in you through the laying on of my hands. For the Spirit God gave us does not make us timid, but gives us power, love and self-discipline. **2 Timothy 1:6-7 (NIV)**

> Each of you should use whatever gift you have received to serve others, as faithful stewards of God's grace in its various forms. **1 Peter 4:10 (NIV)**

Ignorance: You cannot live above your level of knowledge. What you do not know will always limit you. Every problem in the world responds to your knowledge. If you do not know it, you cannot own it. Failure to understand God's success principles cuts you off from Divine provision. Ignorance of the trends in your society robs you of money-making opportunities.

> My people are destroyed from lack of knowledge. "Because you have rejected knowledge, I also reject you as my priests; because you have ignored the law of your God, I also will ignore your children. **Hosea 4:6 (NIV)**

> Therefore my people will go into exile for lack of understanding; those of high rank will die of hunger and the common people will be parched with thirst. **Isaiah 5:13 (NIV)**

Lifestyle Roadblocks

Your life is not determined by your desires but by your choices. Intentions have zero impact on life, only actions matter. Regardless of how noble your goals are, your success boils down to the things you choose to do every day. These choices determine your final outcome. Until goals are assimilated to the point where they affect your moment-by-moment decisions, you will fail.

No Financial Plan and Accountability: If you do not create a plan for it, money spends itself. Money in the hand reveals the hidden desires lying suppressed in the heart. It is easy to control desire when you have no money. Mastering your impulses when you have money in your hands is the way to hold wealth. Most people spend their way into poverty because they cannot manage the desires that flood their minds once they have a little money. Poverty is often caused by spending too much rather than by not earning enough.

> All who are prudent act with knowledge, but fools expose their folly. **Proverbs 13:16 (NIV)**
>
> Plans fail for lack of counsel, but with many advisers they succeed. **Proverbs 15:22 (NIV)**
>
> Suppose one of you wants to build a tower. Won't you first sit down and estimate the cost to see if you have enough money to complete it? For if you lay the foundation and are not able to finish it, everyone who sees it will ridicule you, saying, 'This person began to build and wasn't able to finish.' **Luke 14:28-30 (NIV)**

Laziness: Laziness destroys wealth, as well as health. Laziness can come in the form of excuses, busy work and procrastination. At the heart of laziness are two things; an exaggeration of the difficulty required to do something and the lack of belief in one's ability to do the task. Laziness is the close cousin of fear. A weak heart discovers excuses for postponing action.

> A sluggard buries his hand in the dish; he is too lazy to bring it back to his mouth. **Proverbs 26:15 (NIV)**
>
> A sluggard is wiser in his own eyes than seven people who answer discreetly. **Proverbs 26:16 (NIV)**

Inconsistency: The person who does one thing for a thousand days achieves more than the one who does a thousand things in one day. In order to become exceptional at anything, you must dedicate time and energy to it. The process of failing and getting back up is essential for becoming good at anything. It is required to break in-effective habits of thinking and doing and forming new ones. It is easier to start than it is to finish. The measure of one's mastery over themselves is their ability to repeatedly bring themselves back to the process.

> Such a person is double-minded and unstable in all they do. **James 1:8 (NIV)**

> Turbulent as the waters, you will no longer excel, for you went up onto your father's bed, onto my couch and defiled it. **Genesis 49:4 (NIV)**

<u>Gratification</u>: Your appetite can be your biggest ally or your worst enemy. The person who builds a million dollar enterprise and the one who spends their income on designer clothes have one thing in common. They are both driven by their appetites. The difference between them, however, is where each one places the satisfaction of that desire. The poor man puts pleasure before sacrifice. The rich man puts sacrifice before pleasure. Indulgence destroys wealth, health and happiness.

> Like a city whose walls are broken through is a person who lacks self-control. **Proverbs 25:28 (NIV)**

> For drunkards and gluttons become poor, and drowsiness clothes them in rags. **Proverbs 23:21 (NIV**

CHAPTER ELEVEN: TRUSTING GOD FOR YOUR PAYDAY

Your life is ordered by God. Everything that happens to us as believers plays a role in God's ultimate design for our lives. As long as your heart is in the right place, both the good and the bad events of your life will serve to bring you to the place God planned for you originally. If you do not abort the process by giving up or leaving the path, God is committed to your success and happiness. This is not to say that the bad things that happen to us are God's doing but God will use both the bad and the good for His glory if we remain faithful to Him. When bad things happen to good people, they are usually the result of two things. It could be that the people who are entrusted with responsibility over us fail in their duties. These could be parents, relatives, teachers and government. Trouble also comes from the wrong choices we make. Whatever is the source of our troubles God is greater than them.

The Gateway to Your Payday

> While Jesus was in one of the towns, a man came along who was covered with leprosy. When he saw Jesus, he fell with his face to the ground and begged him, "Lord, if you are willing, you can make me clean." Jesus reached out his hand and touched the man. "I am willing," he said. "Be clean!" And immediately the leprosy left him. **Luke 5:12-13 (NIV)**

Belief is the path of access to anything that God promises us. Without faith it is impossible to connect to the blessings of God. The love and the Power of God are locked away from us if we do not accept His willingness and ability to do the things that He says that He will do. You and I have the power to determine how much power God demonstrates in our lives. Our faith decides whether God is bigger than our challenges or smaller than them. The amount of power that we assign to God is the amount of power that will be available to solve our problems. All the resources heaven has assigned to your life can only reach you through the avenue of your belief. Whatever you do not believe does not exist in your life and therefore cannot make an impact in your experience. The more faith you exercise the more options your life will have and the greater your opportunities for success.

The faith that you need to succeed is two dimensional; you must believe in God and you must believe in yourself. Believing God is also two-dimensional; you have to believe in his willingness to do what you desire and you also have to believe in His ability to do it. The willingness of God deals with his love. If you do not believe that God loves you enough to want you to succeed, you will be unable to ask him anything with boldness. Knowledge of God's love is the key that unlocks the door and gives us unrestricted access to God's presence. Love creates confidence, love creates acceptance and love leads us to relate to God as our Father. Without the love of God firmly fixed in our hearts, we will be hesitant in our request and wonder if we are good enough to receive what we request. Our ability to boldly pursue our desires will be hindered by questions about whether God really wants this for us.

> And hope does not put us to shame, because God's love has been poured out into our hearts through the Holy Spirit, who has been given to us. **Romans 5:5 (NIV)**

> And if we know that he hears us—whatever we ask—we know that we have what we asked of him. **1 John 5:15 (NIV)**

We must also believe in the power of God. Some people believe that God is loving but cannot grasp the fact that He is powerful too. Others know that God is powerful but do not see that He is loving. A loving God without power cannot save us. A powerful God without love will not care about us. Faith in the love and power of God are necessary. Modern life makes it difficult to believe in God's power because we think we have all the answers to the issues of life. We have the solutions to illness, insecurity, natural disaster and danger. There is nothing left for the power of God to do. This is why many believers resort to human efforts to fulfill their destinies. They think that by manipulating things, being smart and hustling hard, they will succeed. When we open the door and admit the supernatural into our lives, we will begin to experience a dimension of life, happiness and success that we never thought possible.

In addition to belief in God, we must believe in ourselves. You are the instrument through which God's purpose will be manifested and you have to believe that you are good enough for God to use. We often limit God's ability to do anything through us to the level of our knowledge and personal history. We think we lack the necessary qualifications. What you and I think of as the reason why God cannot use us is the exact reason why He would. If we were more qualified, we would not feel that we needed Him. The fact that you are not good enough will be the undeniable proof that your success came from God. God could not have claimed glory if He had used a giant to kill Goliath. By using an unarmed teenage boy who was not even a soldier, it was easy to see the involvement of God. What God requires is not our abilities but for us to surrender our inabilities to Him.

The moment you agree with God, He will begin to turn you into the person who can fulfill the purpose that he has in mind. What God demands is your agreement and not your ability. Everyone whom God used in the Bible had to give God their agreement. Afterward that, God took them and began to turn what they considered their weakness into an advantage. Abraham was old and infertile but God brought a nation from his loins. Moses thought He was not good enough but God used him to defeat a superpower. Gideon thought he was the least qualified person in his family but God used him. God is able to do what He promised through you if you are willing to accept His word and recognize that He is not asking you to do anything, only to be the instrument through which He will do everything.

> May he turn our hearts to him, to walk in obedience to him and keep the commands, decrees and laws he gave our ancestors. **1 Kings 8:58 (NIV)**

Avoiding Breakdowns On The Journey

> The Lord had said to Abram, "Go from your country, your people and your father's household to the land I will show you. "I will make you into a great nation, and I will bless you; I will make your name great, and you will be a blessing. I will bless those who bless you, and whoever curses you I will curse; and all peoples on earth will be blessed through you." So Abram went, as the Lord had told him. **Genesis 12:1-4 (NIV)**

There are two things which God requires from us and the absence of which will result in our journey being cut short. The first is faith, which we are already discussing. The other is obedience. If it is God who will achieve what He promised through us, then He requires that we follow His direction at all times. God has a roadmap and He knows the destination. He also knows things about people and our environment which we do not. Oftentimes God will only give us instructions about what to do, He will not explain why. It is only in hindsight that we will realize that the path He led us through was the best one for us. Without trust in God and obedience to his word, you will be unable to walk the path to your payday. Fear will paralyze your ability to act and lead to going in a different direction that the one God wants for you. Resolve in your mind from this moment to give it all it takes; all it takes is to trust and obey God.

> By faith Abraham, when called to go to a place he would later receive as his inheritance, obeyed and went, even though he did not know where he was going. **Hebrews 11:8 (NIV)**

> Abram had become very wealthy in livestock and in silver and gold. **Genesis 13:2 (NIV)**

When we trust and obey God to get us to our payday, He will sometimes lead us in a path that seems to lead away from the goal. There will be inexplicable events that happen in our lives and we will often think that we made a mistake by listening to God. We will even wonder whether we actually heard him at all. Additionally, there will be people who will empower thoughts of doubt in us by asking us why we are facing difficulties if we actually followed God's instructions to us. The only way to get through those situations is through trusting and obeying God more, and not by giving up on our faith. God only shows us glimpses of the destination that He has in mind, but the actual path we must travel to reach it remains with Him. That path is determined by Him based on what the final destination will require. God takes us through detours to prepare and develop us for our destiny.

> He trains my hands for battle; my arms can bend a bow of bronze. You make your saving help my shield; your help has made me great. **2 Samuel 22:35-36 (NIV)**

A lot of the detours that occur on the journey to your payday is for the purpose of developing you. Even though God may pick up an unqualified person for the purpose He has in mind, He does not leave that person the way He found him. Wealth and power require levels of character development and competence that most people do not have. This is why most people will never experience success and wealth. The detours that occur on the road to success are for the purpose of building into us the abilities necessary for managing success when it eventually happens. The more we embrace that process, the more we will be prepared when we get there. There is a period of preparation between the day we say yes to our purpose and the day we arrive at it. That period begins when we start to pursue that purpose in obedience to God's word and under the leading of his Holy Spirit.

It Is A Process

> There is a time for everything, and a season for every activity under the heavens: **Ecclesiastes 3:1 (NIV)**

There are two levels of process within the wealth acquisition journey. The first process is the process of our personal development and growth. The other process is the process of the business growth. Personal wealth and development has many dimensions and the extent to which we surrender to it determines the speed at which the process of business development will proceed. The process of personal development and growth deals with our skills in the areas of self-management which includes how well we manage our emotions, beliefs and desires. It also deals with our management of time. It includes the development of personal knowledge and abilities and the management of our health. Your ability to manage the principal vehicle of your wealth, which is you, will determine the speed at which success happens to you. Your success will not happen apart from your personal development.

> And he sent a man before them—Joseph, sold as a slave. They bruised his feet with shackles, his neck was put in irons, till what he foretold came to pass, till the word of the Lord proved him true. The king sent and released him, the ruler of peoples set him free. He made him master of his household, ruler over all he possessed, **Psalm 105:17-21 (NIV)**

The other aspects of your personal development are your management of relationships and the management of business processes. Wealth cannot be accumulated in isolation, you need other people. Some of these people will be customers, some will be partners, others will be employees and others will be mentors and guides. How well you relate with people determines how much of their personal resources they will release to you; time, money and expertise. The other part is how well you manage your business processes, such as the ability to understand finance or manage technology and facilities. All of these things come together to determine the speed at which you will arrive at success. The road to the payday is a road of constant growth. You must constantly surrender your pride and allow yourself to be taught those things that you do not know. People who refuse to be led into unfamiliar places will never experience the best of God.

Do Not Pull Up Your Seeds

> Let us not become weary in doing good, for at the proper time we will reap a harvest if we do not give up. **Galatians 6:9 (NIV)**

> The one who guards a fig tree will eat its fruit, and whoever protects their master will be honored. **Proverbs 27:18 (NIV)**

Whatever you are doing to reach your payday is a seed. The moment you take action on that goal, you have planted the seed. By continuing to act on it, you are nurturing and watering the seed. Just like a natural seed, the seed of wealth takes time to grow. If you are planting a mushroom, you can expect it to spring up and reach full growth in one night. You have to also remember that mushrooms cannot survive the heat. If you planted the seeds of a tree, you must be prepared to wait. The seed proceeds at its own pace; you may assist it by providing the best conditions but you cannot accelerate it beyond its time. The tree follows its internal timetable and not your own haste. Many people failing to understand this abandon the venture just when it is getting ready to yield results. As long as you keep doing the right things you are making progress, even if it does not look like you are.

There are a number of things that could lead you to pull up your seeds by abandoning your goals. Bear these things in mind.

<u>Failure is part of the process</u>. Failure is proof of progress. When you fail you have just eliminated one unworkable option in your collection of possible solutions. Failure teaches you a lesson that you would never have learned if you did not try. Doing something allows us to test out our assumptions and failure is the feedback from life.

> For though the righteous fall seven times, they rise again, but the wicked stumble when calamity strikes. **Proverbs 24:16 (NIV)**

Discouragement is part of the process. It is the natural process of mourning the death of a foolish assumption. You get discouraged when all your impractical expectations do not come to pass. If you pick yourself up after a discouragement, you do so with an open mind that is willing to learn. Discouragement destroys pride.

> So do not throw away your confidence; it will be richly rewarded. You need to persevere so that when you have done the will of God, you will receive what he has promised. For, "In just a little while, he who is coming will come and will not delay." And, "But my righteous one will live by faith. And I take no pleasure in the one who shrinks back." But we do not belong to those who shrink back and are destroyed, but to those who have faith and are saved. **Hebrews 10:35-39 (NIV)**

Betrayal is the process weeding the wrong people out of your garden. If success was not delayed, some people would not leave your life. Circumstances expose them as being there only to take. If a betrayer takes away an opportunity, have no fear. The opportunity came because of who you are and what you do, if you stay faithful and focused, there will be more opportunities.

> Though my father and mother forsake me, the Lord will receive me. **Psalm 27:10 (NIV)**

Lack can have some valuable lessons to impart. Not having enough money to do what you would teaches you how to use scarce resources to achieve much. It toughens you up and builds the ability to hold on to your goals even in hardship. Lack teaches you to be more creative with the little you have. Without lack you would never learn to reach inside yourself and pull out solutions to problems. You would think money was the answer to all problems.

> He raises the poor from the dust and lifts the needy from the ash heap; he seats them with princes and has them inherit a throne of honor. "For the foundations of the earth are the Lord's; on them he has set the world. **1 Samuel 2:8 (NIV)**

Mistakes reveal a lack of competence. When you make a mistake in something, you tend to go back and reinforce your knowledge in that thing. Mistakes show deficiencies in our knowledge. The trouble with mistakes is that we rue the opportunities we lost. It better to lose an opportunity than to accept it only to lose it to your incompetence.

> But one thing I do: Forgetting what is behind and straining toward what is ahead, **Philippians 3:13b (NIV)**

Wealth building is a process. Many people have stalled in life because they were in a hurry to get rich; they were fooled by a promise of quick and easy wealth. Success requires work; you can put in the work now by building something valuable. Or you can put it in later pretending to be happy and avoiding everyone who actually knows what your life is really like. There are many people who will attempt to discourage you by telling you that it does not work. That is a lie; there are many for whom it is working, you cannot be the exception. If it is not working as planned,

find out what you have been doing wrong and get back to the grind. No place is too small to begin the journey. Joseph started in the prison and Jesus started in the carpenter's shed. The place you begin has no vote in deciding the place where you finish. God is still in the business of taking nobodies and making them Kings.

> A faithful person will be richly blessed, but one eager to get rich will not go unpunished. **Proverbs 28:20 (NIV)**

> He raises the poor from the dust and lifts the needy from the ash heap; **Psalm 113:7 (NIV)**

Make a commitment to begin today. It does not matter if you misused your opportunities in the past, as the saying goes 'better late than never.' The sooner you begin the quicker you will get there; and the earlier you will be able to overwrite the mistakes of the past. However, if you do not take action today, you will be writing your past in indelible ink. Your failures will become final and that is what people will always remember you by. You can't change the past, but you can start changing the future by taking a step today. As you do this, remember that no place is too small to begin if you keep the end in mind. The only wrong place to start from is the place of no action. Also, the struggle is the process of change. Consider the struggle as the exertions of a chick to squeeze out of the egg. Remember that you are the instrument of the process and pay attention to yourself. Finally, never forget that God is in your corner even when you are not. He wants us to reach out to him in Faith, even when our faith has weakened. He wants us to trust him as Job did during his life experiences.

Though he slay me, yet will I trust in him: but I will maintain mine own ways before him. **Job 13:15 (KJV)**

CHAPTER TWELVE: PRAYERS FOR PROSPERITY

Affirmation That God Will Supply My Needs

… hope in God, who richly provides us with everything for our enjoyment. **1 Timothy 6:17b (NIV)**

For every animal of the forest is mine, and the cattle on a thousand hills. **Psalm 50:10 (NIV)**

Heavenly Father, I thank You for Your love and grace over my life. I praise You for Your word which says you give us all things richly to enjoy. I also thank you because you have promised to supply all my need according to Your riches in Christ. Dear Lord, You are the Great God Who made the Heavens and Earth; everything belongs to You. Therefore because my Father owns the cattle on a thousand hills, I will not know lack. I shall not suffer from a lack of money because the God I serve owns the silver and the gold. Where I have had poverty, I call forth prosperity. Where there has been emptiness, I command abundance. In place of pain, I receive gain. My dreams will flourish, my plans shall succeed, my destiny will be assured, and all the desires of my heart will be granted in Jesus name. The money I need will know my name and find my address each day. As I awake this morning, I declare that my life is clean, calm and clear as the early morning dew. My feet are guided and the grace of the Almighty supports and sustains me in all my endeavors. His overflowing goodness supplies my need according to His riches. Thank you Father for answering me, in Jesus name I pray, Amen.

Prayer For Focus and Direction

Whether you turn to the right or to the left, your ears will hear a voice behind you, saying, "This is the way; walk in it." **Isaiah 30:21 (NIV)**

Dear Lord, you promised in Your Words that You guide the steps of a good man. You also said that if I commit my ways to You will bring my desires to pass. Lord, I stretch out my hands today and ask You to guide me. Take my hand and lead me in the direction that is best for me. I open my ears to hear from your Holy Spirit. Lord, give me sensitivity so that I will not be carried away in everyday pursuits that I fail to recognize the urgings of Your Spirit. Give me insight to discern the things that You show to me by through Your word, Your Voice, my dreams, circumstances and the people meet. Lord, I ask you that you set my feet on the path that leads to the prosperity You have prepared for me. In Jesus name I pray, Amen.

Prayer To Discover Your Gifts

The human spirit is the lamp of the Lord that sheds light on one's inmost being. **Proverbs 20:27 (NIV)**

Dear God, to every person in the Bible that you gave a mission, you also gave an instrument for fulfilling that mission. Lord, you have given me a mission to establish your kingdom on earth through the ownership and proper use of material resources. So Father, I ask you today to begin to reveal to me the gifts and abilities planted inside me as the means for carrying out this assignment. Heavenly Father, just as you used the skills of David to bring him into the presence of Saul, guide me to unveil those things in my heart, my mind and my hands that will usher me into my place of honor and greatness. Awaken urgings, memories

and passions in my heart and direct my gaze me to the advantage that you gave to me before I came into this world. This I ask in the precious name of Your Son, Jesus, Amen.

Prayer For Inspired Ideas

> Then Moses cried out to the Lord, and the Lord showed him a piece of wood. He threw it into the water, and the water became fit to drink. **Exodus 15:25a (NIV)**

Dear God, when it was time for David to become the king of Israel, he did not know how to proceed until you spoke an idea to him that sent Him to Hebron. Lord one word from You can save a person from one thousand days of labor. Therefore, I surrender my heart to you and I ask for an idea for success. Heavenly Lord, as I walk on the road, open my eyes to see my world with fresh eyes. When I talk to people, open my ears. In my work and as I eat, let me be aware of those around me and the problems they bear. When I lay down to sleep, open my spirit and reveal needs to me. Fill me with insight for extraordinary results and outstanding impact. Give me an idea that will bring good to people in my generation and beyond. Help me to be the person who sees solutions more than problems. Finally, Lord, give me the wisdom for quick understanding and speedy action. This I pray in Jesus name, Amen.

Prayer For An Enlarged Mind

> I have more understanding than the elders, for I obey your precepts. **Psalm 119:100 (NIV)**

Dear God, you made my mind the door through which You work in my life. Father, I know that a crippled mind hinders and frustrates your purpose in my life. In 2 Timothy 1:7, You say that you give the righteous a mind that is complete in all its faculties. Therefore I affirm that I see and think straight. I have insight and understanding because I have the mind of Christ and I understand all things. Every knowledge and skill that is necessary for success in my career and business I possess. There is nothing beyond my comprehension because I am endowed with insight to pierce the deepest darkness. I have understanding beyond my peers and my teachers through the power of Your Spirit working in my mind. I manifest the wisdom of Joseph and I detect the hidden messages in difficult situations and I devise accurate solutions to them. My mind is freed from every shackle that held it and is enlightened by the word of God, in Jesus name I pray, Amen.

Prayer For Divine Connections

Nations will come to your light, and kings to the brightness of your dawn. "Lift up your eyes and look about you: All assemble and come to you; your sons come from afar, and your daughters are carried on the hip. Then you will look and be radiant, your heart will throb and swell with joy; the wealth on the seas will be brought to you, to you the riches of the nations will come. **Isaiah 60:3-5 (NIV)**

Heavenly Father, guide my feet and lead me to the places where the people who hold the keys to my blessings may be found. Open the roads, the paths, the doors and let all those to whom you have committed my blessings locate me. Lord, when I meet them, they shall recognize me. Before I open my mouth, You will speak to them and they will open their treasures to me. As you sent the Wise Men from the ends of the earth to Bethlehem and they found the Child Jesus, so you will send men to me who will not stop until they find me. I receive the same favor You gave to the children of Israel when they asked the people of Egypt for their wealth. Lord, I thank you for giving me access and acceptance with those who have power to bless me, in Jesus name I pray, Amen.

Prayer For Release From Indebtedness

> For the Lord your God will bless you as he has promised, and you will lend to many nations but will borrow from none. You will rule over many nations but none will rule over you. **Deuteronomy 15:6 (NIV)**

Heavenly Father, I come before Your presence today bringing every burden of debt that has limited my freedom and prevented me from prospering. Lord, I ask forgiveness for every act of mismanagement where I have failed to diligently manage the resources You committed to my care. Forgive me for squandering Your money on things that I did not need and bringing myself under the power of the creditor through acts of financial recklessness. Lord, Your word says that the borrower is a slave to the lender and it is not Your will for my life to be under the control of another person. Therefore, I pledge today to become more responsible with my money and to live within my means. I ask you to extend grace to me and help me get out of my current situation. Lord, give me the wisdom to speak with those to whom I am indebted. Give me the self-discipline to manage my money properly. Most of all help me to find a plan through which I can begin to build a store of wealth and lend to others. This I ask in Jesus name, Amen.

The Prayer of Jabez

> Jabez was a good man whose goodness was not reflected in the results that he got. He prayed to God for a turnaround in his circumstances and God heard him. Jabez was

more honorable than his brothers. His mother had named him Jabez, saying, "I gave birth to him in pain." Jabez cried out to the God of Israel, "Oh that you would bless me and enlarge my territory! Let your hand be with me, and keep me from harm so that I will be free from pain." And God granted his request. **1 Chronicles 4:9-10 (NIV)**

You may be like Jabez; caught in a spiritual struggle that is not of your own making. If you feel as if you are fighting a spiritual battle for wealth and things never work out despite your best efforts, you may be in the same situation as Jabez and should pray this prayer.

Heavenly Father, I come to You today through the work of Your Son Jesus, when He shed His blood for me on the cross. Lord, Your word says that whatever a man sows that is what he will reap. That if a thief is caught, he will restore what he has stolen sevenfold. Upon these words I declare that the enemy has no right over my property and prosperity. I declare that I will eat the fruit of my labor and I will not labor for the fire. I stand in the name of Jesus to rebuke every force of darkness that acts as a devourer in my life. You shall no longer have access to my wealth and my happiness. I put an end to your operations in the life of me and my family, in Jesus name. Heavenly Father, Your word says that Jabez called to You and You granted his request. Dear Lord, I also call upon You; bless me and enlarge my territory. Let Your hand be with me and keep me from harm so that I will be free from pain. Lord, I believe that You have heard me and I receive my answers in Jesus name, Amen.

CHAPTER THIRTEEN: PAYDAY CONFESSION SCRIPTURES

These Bible verses are for affirmation of what the word of God has said about you and your wealth. They contain promises of divine health, wealth and protection. Speak them daily over yourself, your business and your family. Build them into your heart and make them a part of your daily walk with God. Confess these words aloud until they become embedded in your consciousness.

Affirmations for Everyday Success

> May those who delight in my vindication shout for joy and gladness; may they always say, "The Lord be exalted, who delights in the well-being of his servant." **Psalm 35:27 (NIV)**

> For you know the grace of our Lord Jesus Christ, that though he was rich, yet for your sake he became poor, so that you through his poverty might become rich. **2 Corinthians 8:9 (NIV)**

I boldly declare boldly that it is your will that I prosper. I have a right to prosper because wealth has been assigned to me by the grace of My Lord and Savior Jesus who exchanged His wealth for my poverty.

> Beloved, I pray that you may prosper in all things and be in health, just as your soul prospers. **3 John 2 (NKJV)**

Your desire for me is health, wellbeing and prosperity. I banish sickness and disease from my body, family and habitation. I call upon wealth. I call upon health. I call upon happiness. I declare my doors open to all good things.

> Blessed is the one who does not walk in step with the wicked or stand in the way that sinners take or sit in the company of mockers, but whose delight is in the law of the Lord, and who meditates on his law day and night. That person is like a tree planted by streams of water, which yields its fruit in season and whose leaf does not wither—whatever they do prospers. **Psalm 1:1-3 (NIV)**

Because I am the righteous who does not walk in the way of the wicked, I declare also that I am the blessed who prospers in everything that I do. My effort yields success as a tree planted by the river of water. I am full of life and I overflow in encouragement to people around me. My leaves shall be a shade and people shall seek out my presence. My life is full of God's strength. I am not defeated, but I am prospering in my mind, in my body, in my spirit, and my finances. I flourish in my marriage, family and relationships. Whatever I do prospers.

> Give and it will be given to you. A good measure, pressed down, shaken together and running over, will be poured into your lap. For with the measure you use, it will be measured to you." **Luke 6:38 (NIV)**

> And my God will meet all your needs according to the riches of his glory in Christ Jesus. **Philippians 4:19 (NIV)**

I have given and it is being continually given back to me in overflowing measures by men, women and nations. I receive measures of goodwill, measures of open doors, measures of opportunities and measures of financial prosperity. Everything abounds to me in good measure, pressed down, shaken together, and running over.

> Bring the whole tithe into the storehouse, that there may be food in my house. Test me in this," says the Lord Almighty, "and see if I will not throw open the floodgates of heaven and pour out so much blessing that there will not be room enough to store it. **Malachi 3:10 (NIV)**

By my obedience to your command to tithe my income, the floodgates of heaven are opened over me and I am receiving more blessing than I have room to contain. The devourer is rebuked for my sake. I sow little and reap much because the mercy of God covers my deficiencies.

> Surely, Lord, you bless the righteous; you surround them with your favor as with a shield. **Psalm 5:12 (NIV)**

> The Lord make his face shine on you and be gracious to you; the Lord turn his face toward you and give you peace.'" **Numbers 6:25-26 (NIV)**

I confess that I walk in God's favor today in all my business dealings and with all people with whom I will meet. The favor of God will shield me and all who belong to me in the face of danger and death. He makes His face to shine upon me, therefore my face shines and people love me because of God's presence that goes with me. I will encounter peace and not war because God goes before me to open up the hard places. I have God's favor and blessing on me. I am a success today.

> "'If you can'?" said Jesus. "Everything is possible for one who believes." **Mark 9:23 (NIV)**

I expect possibilities today. God will make a way for me through the impassable sea and the hard rock will yield water to me. I walk forward expecting answers. Where I have been rejected in the past, I will be invited. And my words will open the prison doors of wealth.

> You will be blessed when you come in and blessed when you go out. The Lord will grant that the enemies who rise up against you will be defeated before you. They will come at you from one direction but flee from you in seven. **Deuteronomy 28:6-7 (NIV)**

I am blessed in my coming in and in my going out. The Lord sends the Angel of His presence before me to disperse every gathering of evildoers. I walk with goodness and mercy behind me. The sun will not smite me but will be a light. Disease shall find me because the Lord is my healer. Arrows of death will not come near me and my loved ones because the blood of Jesus speaks on our behalf. We shall go forth in joy and return in peace.

> Christ redeemed us from the curse of the law by becoming a curse for us, for it is written: "Cursed is everyone who is hung on a pole." **Galatians 3:13 (NIV)**

Yes, indeed Jesus has redeemed me from the curse of lack. I am blessed because of Him! I shall not lack spiritually. I shall not lack emotionally. I shall not lack materially. I shall not lack in my health. Redeemed, redeemed, I am redeemed, highly favored and thoroughly blessed.

I declare and affirm all these to be true by the unbreakable word of God, in Jesus name, Amen.

About The Author

Yolanda Washington-Cowan is a wife and mom first. She is the CEO of B-Inspired Publishing Company, as well as an author under her label. She is also the founder and President of B-Inspired.Org, a Non-Profit Organization that helps women to break free from the poverty trap. Through its job-readiness training, career development, and job placement programs, B-Inspired.Org helps these women realize their full potential and achieve financial stability.

Yolanda grew up in Memphis, Tennessee. In this book; ***Every Day Is A Payday In God's Kingdom***, she teaches principles derived from her personal struggles trying to escape a life of poverty. In it she explains simple lessons anyone can use to make their finances better.

She is an upcoming author who connects with readers by sharing life experiences and Biblical principles that beautyfully illustrate how God changes lives when people learn to trust Him, seek His will, and follow His lead, no matter their circumstances.

She fellowships at a church under an Apostolic Ministry and faithfully serves on the Teacher Ministry, a member of the Book ministry and is part of the Women Group Life ministry in her church. She regularly connects with her Christian sisters on a daily prayer line that helps them stay in touch through praying and intercession.

Her other books are '**Gracefully Broken**', '**Diamonds in the Rough**', '**50 Motivational Prayers for Financial Break-through and Devine Healing**', '**10 Ways to Become Debt Free**' and she has more Spirit-filled titles coming out soon.

www.ingramcontent.com/pod-product-compliance
Lightning Source LLC
Chambersburg PA
CBHW051802040426
42446CB00007B/475